The Lost City: Old Aberdeen

The Lost City: Old Aberdeen

Jane Stevenson and Peter Davidson

PHOTOGRAPHY BY *David Langan*
with Marie Shaw and Eric Ellington

EDITED BY *Marc Ellington and Daniel MacCannell*

First published in 2008 by
Birlinn Limited
West Newington House
10 Newington Road
Edinburgh
EH9 1QS

www.birlinn.co.uk

Hardback
ISBN13: 978 1 84158 738 7
ISBN10: 1 84158 738 9

Paperback
ISBN13: 978 1 84158 813 1
ISBN10: 1 84158 813 X

British Library Cataloguing-in-Publication Data
A catalogue record for this book is available
from the British Library

Designed and typeset by Mark Blackadder

Endpaper: John Slezer, 'The Prospect of Old Aberdien',
Theatrum Scotiae (1693)

Printed and bound in Slovenia

Contents

Foreword

Marc Ellington of Towie Barclay DL

The 'Lost City' of Old Aberdeen is one of Scotland's greatest but least known treasures. From the fifteenth century, the ancient burgh on the Don was legally autonomous from the newer bustling trading-town on the Dee. Therefore it is not a suburb of its larger neighbour but a miniature city, with its own distinct trades, institutions and traditions. Old Aberdeen is and has always been much loved by those who have lived here, been educated here, or simply fallen under its spell. King's College Chapel, with its crown spire, the magnificent Georgian Town House, familiar from its use as the logo of the Architectural Heritage Society of Scotland, and St Machar's Cathedral, with its massive twin towers, are among the iconic buildings of our nation, yet remain little known to those who have no personal connection with either the Old Town or the university.

A walk in Old Aberdeen will take you through an anthology of Scottish building from the Middle Ages to the present day; a delicately layered townscape of exceptional beauty and historic interest. There is much to delight the visitor as well as valuable lessons to be learned.

The burgh grew up around its great cathedral, developing into a university city in the sixteenth century due to the vision of one of Scotland's greatest statesmen, Bishop William Elphinstone. As Old Aberdeen was the creation of a Renaissance man who saw practical improvement and intellectual development as partners, not opposites, the Reformation, when it came, was a gentler process here than elsewhere. The university and the community it served were an island of tolerance in intolerant times: Catholics, Episcopalians and Presbyterians contrived ways of living with one another's claims to spiritual authority while each remaining passionately convinced of the value of their own. As such, an example to today's multi-cultural Scotland.

The architectural history and evolution of Old Aberdeen reflect a more balanced and 'natural' progression than that of most other Scottish cities. The result is a triumph of casually-evolved organic town-planning and development; a university city, which has over the centuries grown and gracefully absorbed a wide variety of private houses, shops and academic buildings to create a single, integrated community of great character, charm and atmosphere.

This book is an invitation to wander through a microcosm of urban Scotland at its best, with masterpieces of medieval masonry on one hand

and humble eighteenth-century cottages on the other. There are treasures and surprises at every turn, and a wealth of buildings offering outstanding examples of Scottish architectural design and detailing from many periods. The journey to discover the 'Lost City' of Old Aberdeen has much to teach us about our past and how we once lived; it can also, I believe, serve as an inspiration and a pattern for the Scotland of the future.

Recollections of Old Aberdeen

Professor C. Duncan Rice, Principal and Vice-Chancellor, University of Aberdeen

Some forty-five years ago it was my habit to take lunch daily in the St Machar Bar. It was a real crossroad between the university and town communities, but only in a very limited way. Although we had already moved into the age of smart plastic bars the St Machar had been forgotten by time. There were no seats, except for two upturned beer crates by the gas fire, for which there was eager competition. There was also a bench down the left-hand side of the room opposite the domino tables. The bar was rigidly all male, perhaps because of the limitation imposed by a single pissoir which was little more than a black waist-high wall.

I say limited because, at least in the middle of the day, the regular attendees were few. One who influenced me greatly was Jim Noble, or 'Flash' – thus nicknamed because he was town lamplighter in the last years of the gas lights. The barman, also Jim, soon revealed that if we bought an entire pint of beer, drank two-thirds of it, and subsequently asked for a half-pint, he would fill the pint glass up to the top. This seemed an admirable economy, and justified spending whatever money was available on beer instead of solid food. The St Machar didn't have solid food anyway. We were a tiny handful of students. There were only two academic patrons – W.

Douglas Simpson, the archaeologist/ librarian; and Ronnie Ireland, a legal scholar who subsequently had a distinguished career as Sheriff. He had a fine wet-nosed spaniel.

I don't know if that means that the St Machar in the good old days was better or worse than it is now. But we certainly solved most of the world's problems in it, and, when lunch was extended, we occasionally returned to the old library in King's Quad – now the Conference Centre – to interrupt the studies of our friends and be chided by the sacrist's noise constables.

The library we are building at the university will be a little different; but I know it will be more welcoming to the people and children of Old Aberdeen than its predecessor was. In the meantime, there are still wonderful crossovers between the university and the lost city. Just before Christmas every year we gather in the cathedral, with the great heraldic ceiling blurred by the dusk above, and the squat Norman pillars hemming in the packed pews. It's not a service the first bishops would have been comfortable with, but it pulls together as nothing else does the triangle between town, church and college that inspired Elphinstone.

Elphinstone and Hector Boece are still very much with us. They shared much of the

cosmopolitanism and public commitment we strive for in the modern university. Elphinstone was educated in Glasgow, Paris, and Orléans; Boece in Dundee and at the Sorbonne with Erasmus. Both returned to serve their country and worked together to found an extraordinary institution which, Peter Davidson and Jane Stevenson tell us, has since expanded by 64,000 per cent.

We still use the chapel on the Sunday mornings of high holidays. I sit in a Renaissance stall carved with Scottish thistles and continental vine leaves, and covered with graffiti from eighteenth-century students. That always makes me think what it's all about. I will never forget leaving the chapel once with a very senior colleague who turned to me in the procession to whisper, 'Christ, if we all get this wrong we're going to burn in hell!'

None of my family lived in Old Aberdeen, although all of them came from Aberdeenshire or Kincardineshire, and all the modern ones lived in the city. But one of my earliest visual recollections was my parents' wedding picture, which I imagined to be taken at King's, although it probably wasn't. And of course there were many other relatives who had been at the university, and many who had been married in the chapel. A small number are in the remembrance book.

So I came up as a student, a child of the west-end bourgeoisie, not knowing Old Aberdeen. It changed my life. All the visual resonances have stayed with me wherever I have gone – the curious slabbed cathedral towers sticking up over the trees at the edge of Seaton Park; the exhilarating flair of the widening cobbles between St Mary's and the Town House; the long march of the Chanonry, where Grierson lived and Janet Adam Smith was brought up; lamplight in the rain on the flagstones outside King's courtyard. And now there are newer visual flashes that mean King's to me – the nickel sheen on the split apple held by by Kenny Hunter's androgynous boy where students have put their hand to feel the pips; the harsh medieval painting of the restored escutcheons above the chapel buttresses; the round recess in the law school yard where they do poetry readings at Word, clustered round Dilworth's armadillo; and the serene astrolabe and mosaics of the MacRobert memorial.

So much has changed. The office where I sit as I write this preface was, when I was a boy, a hockey field. Even Reginald Jones's physics building, which was new long ago, is being expanded to put a new Institute of Mathematical Sciences at the back. And the new library and various other projects will turn the landward campus upside down so that it becomes an echo of what Elphinstone built, divided from it by the great artery of the medieval main street.

It was magical then, and it's magical now. Jane and Peter don't say so, but at least for me, at a lower level of information than them, we live in one of the most extraordinary streetscapes in Europe. And the little college Elphinstone founded has become a world-class university – which is exactly what he would have wished for it as he struggled to bring Scotland and his own diocese right out on the European frontier, close to the metropolitan world of Paris and Rome.

I often wonder, from my point of agnostic disadvantage, what cosmic plan gave me the honour and joy of working here. I have never felt that as strongly as after reading the manuscript for this wonderful book. I commend it to all.

CHAPTER ONE

A Walk Northward Through the Lost City

The noise of traffic from the roundabout falls behind as soon as you turn into King's Crescent. Stone tenements on the right; backlands, vacant lots, stonemasons' yards and depots behind metal fences beyond them. These were once the debatable lands between the two distinct burghs of New and Old Aberdeen. Now, gusts of rain flicker through floodlights on winter evenings as the lamps come on in the windows of the colour-washed villas opposite. The front gardens slope sharply up from the pavement as cottages give way to the reversing curve of the bay-windowed, haunted, concrete-built terrace. The slope to the left grows steeper still in front of the late-Victorian rectory, St Margaret's Brae, in which esteemed architect Sir Ninian Comper (see box, p.2) spent his childhood. It is simple and substantial, the disposition of the façade organised on lines familiar throughout Scotland: flat-fronted, three broad bays rising into dormers which break the roof-line. The panels which frame first-floor windows and dormers carry memories of castles along the Dee and throughout the hinterland of Aberdeenshire, but the recollection is subtle and simple, transformed by the medium. The material, finish and detail are characteristically Aberdonian. Silver granite is smoothed and expertly jointed; ornament is implied only with shadow and the fall of the light on shallow raised courses of squared stone.

Trees thicken behind the wall that marches with the pavement, and amidst their branches the ground rises abruptly to a spine of rock crowned with a soaring, perpendicular church: high gables and red-pantiled dormers are half-visible amidst the leaves. Concealment and height add to the power and fantasy of Comper's first completed work, one which was already, in the early 1890s when the architect had much of his long career ahead of him, a manifestation of his lifelong vision for High Episcopalian and Anglo-Catholic architecture and a historicist aesthetic that rewrites history.

The initial impression from the street is of Comper's adroitness in his use of the site. Like all powerfully imagined buildings, it gives an impression of massiveness despite its comparatively modest size. Only the chapel and the first bay of the projected buildings were finished, and the northern end of the row is still composed of one-and-a-half-storey granite 'Captains' houses' adapted for the use of the convent. From their upper rooms the sea is within sight. This could be no other city in Scotland but Aberdeen.

Comper's terms of reference in his chapel are Scots and Flemish, a vision of a Scottish Gothic

St Margaret's Convent.

Above. A lost city's lost locomotive, Seaton Park.

Opposite. Don Street: once the only road to Balgownie and its vital bridge.

Sir Ninian Comper and the Society of St Margaret

St Margaret's Convent owes its origins to a meeting between two men: the Rev. John Comper, who became rector of St John's Episcopal Church in 1861, and J.M. Neale, a clergyman of the Church of England, who combined deep scholarship with a direct, practical interest in caring for the poor and unfortunate. Neale was also one of the Church of England's greatest hymn-writers, responsible for some of the most cherished of Christmas carols, 'Good King Wenceslas', 'O Come O Come Emmanuel', and 'A Great and Mighty Wonder'.

In 1854, Neale was one of the founders of the Society of St Margaret, an order of Anglican nuns dedicated to tending the poor and sick in their own homes. Comper was deeply impressed by this vision of practical Christianity, and invited Neale to Aberdeen to discuss the possibility of establishing a similar community in the North. When Sister

Zillah from Neale's original foundation at East Grinstead arrived in Aberdeen in 1862 – the first Anglican nun ever to set foot there – she moved in with the Comper family and the seed was sown. When other women were attracted to the work and the life, the little community moved into a house near St John's. Comper founded St Margaret's Church in the Gallowgate, a deliberate move into the slums of New Aberdeen.

By 1871, the mission had progressed to the point where it was necessary to seek permanent premises for an Episcopalian sisterhood. A pair of recently built cottages with surrounding lands on the Spital came on the market in 1874, and seemed promising. The Rev. Comper began to build.

One of Comper's daughters became a sister of St Margaret's. But he also had a son who had left home to begin his professional life by the time the project began. Neale was

the boy's godfather, and his name was Ninian, later Sir Ninian Comper (1864–1960). He would become the architect of some of the boldest and best churches of the nineteenth century, a master of the so-called Gothic Revival. His work has also been described as 'the apogee of all that is best about the Christian art of the twentieth century'.

Sir Ninian's distinguished career began with St Margaret's. His view of the project is probably best summed up with these words, which he wrote in 1917: 'The purpose of a church is not to express the age in which it was built, or the individuality of its designer. Its purpose is to move to worship, to bring a man to his knees, to refresh his soul in a weary land.' Thus for Sir Ninian, every commission for church architecture was glorious. All of his buildings were intended to move and delight, and to make it easy and natural to praise God.

church, like the Holy Rude at Stirling, furnished and maintained as it might have been in the early sixteenth century. Inside, the conjuring with space continues: verticality and the soaring window at the east end give a sense of vastness within a modest compass. The detailing is flawless: the coloured and gilded reredos, the tall stone sacrament-house with its figure of the Virgin, the finely detailed stone balcony for the Mother Superior above the stalls. The plain, limewashed walls contrast with the painted boarding of the ceiling: stylised carnations, like those on Byzantine silks or oriental rugs, in sea green and faded rose add an element of richness, a reminiscence of the tempera-painted ceilings and white walls of rooms in the tower houses of Scotland. The whole ensemble is unforgettable,

especially with the level sunlight of winter striking the gilding through watery leaded glass.

The consecration of the chapel is described in the recollections of one of the founding sisters, whose memory is much coloured by Comper's virtuosity in conjuring a spacious interior from such a constricted site:

Looking down from the organ gallery at Vespers that evening, on the black and white veils of the sisters, the lofty vaults of the tower among which the flickering shadows were playing – the dim outline of the tall vast windows – and the gorgeous colouring of the reredos, which was lighted by the rays of the setting sun; it was difficult to realise that only a wall

*separated us from the busy, hurrying life
of the nineteenth century.*

But even now, walking the rising slope, there is a
feeling of a movement away from the noise of
the city. St Martha's, another vertical building on
the spine of rock to the left, combines the L-plan
and stair-tower of a modest castle with detailing
taken from Scottish ecclesiastical Gothic. It was
originally built by the Rev. John Comper, father
of Sir Ninian, as a home for women workers in
nearby factories; just one manifestation of his
boundless concern for the more vulnerable
members of Aberdeen society.

On the right, at the brow of the hill, is the
first substantial stone villa standing in the

remains of its extensive gardens, much altered
and extended in the nineteenth and early
twentieth centuries, but still keeping its long
garden wall and pedimented gate, a foretaste of
the spacious villas and manses of Old Aberdeen.
It also reminds us of the long years during which
these territories between the two towns were
open space: nursery gardens and sparse (albeit
grand) houses, traversed by the miry north-
bound road. The old way is traced by the
modern street – still, incredibly, called the Spital
after St Peter's Hospital, gone now these three
centuries.

Standing at the top of the rise, a backward
glance south frames the modern city centre with
stone buildings and fine trees: the slab of flats on

the Gallowgate and the towers beyond, the granite needle of Marischal College, the fortalice of the Citadel, the lead spire of the Town House. The prospect composes in a way that is barely Scots, far less British, leading the mind inevitably to the cold cities with which Aberdeen once traded, across the North Sea and over to the Baltic.

A street plunges down to the right, mostly typical Aberdeen granite tenements, three broad bays wide, central chimney above the central door: a distinct echo of the burgh houses of early-modern Scotland, an index of the northern reluctance to abandon an idea or style that works, however outmoded it may seem to the nervous south. In the distance are the brave red seats of Pittodrie stadium and beyond it the strand and the sea. The flash of red is a fine, defiant statement, especially when slate-grey clouds muster behind it.

Ahead is the level backbone of the Spitalhill. On the right, a jumble of harled public housing reminds us of the post-war era's honest attempt to replace the tattered patchwork of buildings that had arisen in this gap between New and Old Aberdeen. The houses to the left are high, many placed on the ridge to catch the view out to the links and the shore. Pleasing details abound: a first-floor balcony-rail in elegant wrought iron; two symmetrical shops built to frame the forecourt of an eighteenth-century house with a finely eccentric disposition of windows in the gable-end it shows to the street. Bordering the pavement are the premises of what was a splendid second-hand bookshop, remembered with affection for its judicious balance of the random and the ordered, the vintage scents of binder's glue and tobacco, the piles of prints. Its long, horizontal windows (themselves a distin-

guished example of the shopfitter's art) retain their neatly lettered advertisements of the departments of knowledge formerly for sale within, preserved after it was converted into dwellings.

Down a slope to the right is the entrance to the graveyard which, from 1830, has occupied the lands of the old church of the Spital. This is a magnificent garden-cemetery with details of consistent quality: the lodges are solidly classical, shading into Egyptian; the burial enclosure of the Moirs of Scotstoun matches the accustomed massive gravity of Scottish funerary architecture; the cast-iron gates are magnificent in their weight and poise. But all of this is only the context for the grass and the trees, the movement of leaves and shadows over as fine an assemblage of granite monuments – obelisks and draped urns – as can be imagined.

Returning to the Spital itself, the eye is once more led up to the high spine of the rock opposite to a pleasantly solid granite cottage placed on the last of the ridge; a vertiginous front garden connects it with the street. The main road begins to slope downwards. For a few hundred yards, the distinctive atmosphere of the northern city is diluted by a more general feeling of urban Scotland in high tenements and the etched-glass pub windows of the Red Lion, 'the Beastie', successor of a more expansive ancient inn of the same name on the other side of the road. In the eighteenth century, when Old Aberdeen's King's College and New Aberdeen's Marischal College were wholly separate universities, the Wise Club or Aberdeen Philosophical Society, which drew its membership from both, met in this no-man's-land between the towns.

There is another second-hand bookshop, still trading, on the right. Once, on the third of

January, that curious day between the years when Scotland is, in the words of the poet Eliot, 'living and partly living', a day of wind-driven sleet and early dark, the lights of the shop were shining out, almost the only sign of life in the whole city. Inside there were crisp 1930s Ordnance Survey maps mounted on linen to be had for a few pounds, and the chance to browse the Spalding Club's old volumes of Aberdeenshire and Moray history amid a selection (like Old Aberdeen itself) distinctively local but consistently international. There was an extraordinary hour of peace, reading about forgotten quarrels and past risings in the warm, deserted bookshop, with not a single figure battling along the snowy pavement through the pool of light from the windows.

On the opposite corner is a genial takeaway called the Khyber Pass. It has given its name to the entire corner by some process of osmosis. Inside, the overhead television seems always to be showing a cricket match. Whether this is coincidence, or whether there is a subscription channel somewhere that shows only cricket matches, is a very minor mystery of Old Aberdeen which has yet to be resolved.

The surface of the roadway changes from tarmac to cobble at this narrow point in the street. A crossroads, parked cars and stationary bins offer a daily obstacle course to the skills of the élite corps who drive the number twenty, Old Aberdeen's only bus, which shuttles up and down the old Royal Highway between Marischal College and Hillhead of Seaton, taking in the whole length of the ancient burgh.

From the western pavement, the first classic view of the heart of Old Aberdeen now unfolds at your feet: the long curve of the Georgian houses of College Bounds, their doors opening

Above. The old Red Lion Inn, where the Aberdeen Philosophical Society met in the eighteenth century.

Opposite. Charles 'Priest' Gordon, 1772–1855.

directly onto the granite-cobbled street. Some of their roofs still have the pantiles which originally distinguished them, and whose warm colour remained long in the memory of Aberdeen graduates of years past – the orange of the roofs echoing the red gowns of the students passing up the hill between the grey houses.

The trees of the first professorial manse hang over its high garden wall on the left. Here too we

catch a first sight of the roofs and monumental chimneys of the tall Georgian manses at the southern corner of King's College itself. Beyond them is the pivot – physical and emotional – of the whole place: the crown spire of the college's late-fifteenth-century chapel, holding aloft on four ribbed arches a drum surmounted by the closed imperial crown of the kings of Scots. In the thin bright air of spring, on the first soft day when every view seems to end in leaves or the sea, it seems to gather the light into itself.

As the hill slopes downwards, the former bank, now a dignified mosque, is on the right. Descending the curving slope, the sense of entering an enclave, an old settlement, a lost city, is very strong. Almost everything now visible, with few exceptions, is Georgian or early-Victorian, but the preservation of layout and street-plan, what might be called the essential rhythm of the city, is complete. The atmosphere of retiredness and tranquillity, which marked the Old Town from the nineteenth century, is still apprehensible. The right-hand side of College Bounds is a harmonious succession of granite houses of the eighteenth and nineteenth centuries, mostly of three or five bays and two storeys with attic dormers. On the left, after an unambitious little park, houses give way to the high garden wall of the Research Institute for Irish and Scottish Studies – until recently, a manse assigned to the King's professor of Latin, and still known as Humanity Manse. The wall's expanse is broken by the Institute's modern arched entrance and, further down, by the blocked gateway to the Church of Our Lady of the Snows, founded by William Elphinstone (bishop of Aberdeen 1482–1514) and known as the Snow Kirk (see box, p.8). The blocked gateway, with Elphinstone's mitre-crowned arms above, long gave the house the name of The Sign of the Mitre.

Humanity Manse, sheltered by the slope of the hill to the south, is a four-square villa, three bays by three bays, on two floors with attic dormers. The old professorial manses (and the town houses of the gentry, which resemble them so closely) almost all accord to the same essential layouts of both façade and ground plan, but

The Snow Kirk

Like so much else in Old Aberdeen, the Snow Kirk owes its origin to Bishop Elphinstone. We can only guess why Elphinstone chose Our Lady of the Snows as the dedicatee of his new church (a dedication shared by a remote, secret Catholic church at Corgaff, far away in the wilds of Strathdon). Its haunting name is an evocation of his personal devotion to the Virgin, and his memories of Rome. In the late autumn of 1494 he began the long journey to the Pope's city, not only to present a formal report on the state of his diocese, but also with the private aim of persuading Pope Alexander VI to approve his project of founding a university. Having entered the wintry city through the Flaminian Gate, like all travellers from the north, he will have found it in the middle of a thorough Renaissance overhaul: St Peter's had been rebuilt in 1452, and the Sistine Chapel was even then under way. It was not the Vatican, however, but one of the city churches which spoke most personally to Elphinstone, Santa Maria Maggiore (Great St Mary's), also known as Santa Maria ad Nives. It was already a thousand years old when Elphinstone saw it, its vast interior glittering with early-Christian mosaics in dim, rich colour; the Virgin herself, throned in splendour but with a sweet and pensive face, looks down from the apse.

This Roman church owed its origin, so legend said, to a vision. The Virgin appeared to Pope Liberius one night in the year 352, and told him that he must build her a church on a precise area of the Esquiline Hill, which would be defined by a snowfall the following morning. Despite the sweltering heat of an Italian August, the marvelling citizens woke to find an extensive snowfall on the Esquiline, the boundaries of which they marked out forthwith. By Elphinstone's time, it had become one of the four most important churches in Rome. Alexander VI was in the process of further adorning the church by gilding its coffered ceiling with the first gold to reach Europe from the New World: the gift of Ferdinand and Isabella of Spain.

When Old Aberdeen became a burgh of barony in 1489, its new status and dignity required it to have a parish church of its own, 'with bell-tower, bell, cemetery, place for holy things, baptismal font, and other things proper to a parochial church'. No matter that the residents were all of half a mile from the substantial St Machar's Cathedral and their working days were already punctuated by the booming bells of King's College Chapel. Dating from 1498, the parish boundaries for this new church specifically excluded the canons of St Machar's who were to continue to attend services in the cathedral.

The great Roman original was a city church, and Old Aberdeen was, technically speaking, a miniature city. Elphinstone's personal devotion to Mary is indicated by his seal, with the Virgin in pride of place; by the dual dedication of the cathedral (which before the Reformation was the church of St Mary and St Machar); and by the dedication of the college, which, according to its common seal, was the College of St Mary, not King's. It was the Virgin that Elphinstone turned to 'in vigils with sighs and groans', as he said in a charter of 1499, when the amount of responsibility he had taken on temporarily daunted him.

It may be that the bleak winters of Aberdeenshire made Elphinstone think that those who worshipped at his new foundation would often trudge there through the snow, but it may also be the case that in naming the modest building after one of the greatest basilicas in Christendom, he revealed something of the tremendous ambition and energy of his vision for Old Aberdeen.

The burgh's church of Our Lady of the Snows was dedicated in 1503, and two small bells called Schochtmadony and Skellat were taken from the south-west turret of St Machar's and gifted to the new foundation by the bishop and cathedral clergy. Priestly services were first provided by Walter Boece, brother of the historian Hector, and, subsequently, by one of the professors of the college (all of whom were in holy orders before the Reformation). But it was to serve the people of Old Aberdeen for less than a hundred years. The post-Reformation Church of Scotland annexed the cathedral, and the Snow Kirk, though not actually demolished, was left to fall down. Plain and small, a simple rectangle with crow-step gables and no tower, there was nothing about its appearance to attract the wrath of the reformers. The building survived for another hundred years or so.

The Snow Kirk, neglected and discredited as it was, maintained a secret life of its own, as did the 'Spittal kirk' (i.e., the church on the Spital which served the leper hospital of St Peter's, first mentioned in 1333 and suppressed in 1427, when its revenues were transferred to the cathedral). In the seventeenth century, the Reformed Kirk enjoined that 'the parochinneris of Snaw and Spittal be compellit to resort to the said kirk of Machar to heir thair the evangel [gospel] preichit, the sacraments ministrat and discipline exercisit, as their awin proper parochin in time to cum', and gave 'power to the said college of Aberdene to dimoleishe and tak doun the ruinous walls and tymber of the present kirkis of Snaw and Spittal now abusit to superstition and idolatrie'. William Guild, the energetic principal of King's who took office in 1640, did just that: with the college desperately in need of repair, he raided the Snow Kirk, or perhaps its outbuildings, for cut stone, 'whereat many Oldtown people murmured, the same being sometime the parish kirk of Old Aberdeen, within the whilk their friends and forefathers were buried'. John Slezer's view of Old Aberdeen, from 1693 (see

The Snow Kirk today.

endpapers), shows the Snow Kirk still standing.

What was 'superstition and idolatrie', or an undue concern with the dead, to the Reformed Kirk might be seen by others as legitimate religious expression; a century and a half was quite long enough to create obstinate attachments. The people of the Old Town, stubbornly conservative, did not value the Snow Kirk because it was crypto-Catholic, but merely because it was theirs. King's, chronically short of money, also clung to its ancient rights. Far from completing the 'dimoleishing' of the Snow Kirk, Guild's successors saw it as an asset in

itself: in 1671, they began to charge £8 Scots for burial in the church and 'ane dollar' for burial in the cemetery beyond the walls. The Catholic church maintained a stronger hold on Aberdeenshire than it did in the south of the country and, over time, the Snow Kirk, ruinous, but not desecrated, became a place of sepulchre for northern Catholics.

Bishop James Grant, vicar apostolic of the Lowlands vicariate (one of the two divisions of the eighteenth-century Catholic church in Scotland), was one of the first such, and he shares a grave with a successor, Bishop John

Geddes, who died in 1799. Geddes's nephew Charles 'Priest' Gordon, builder of the Catholic cathedral and an immensely popular figure in Aberdeen, was laid in the same tomb, fifty-six years later, after the Catholic Emancipation Act.

Today, the Snow Kirk stands reduced to the remains of its four walls, but it is still there. A secret, winding path leads from Powis Gate to the graveyard, a serene and peaceful spot which few even know to exist: a distillation of Scottish Catholic history in a single quiet precinct. It is still in use as a Catholic graveyard.

Right. Gates leading to the house known as Powis Gate.

Far right. College Bounds.

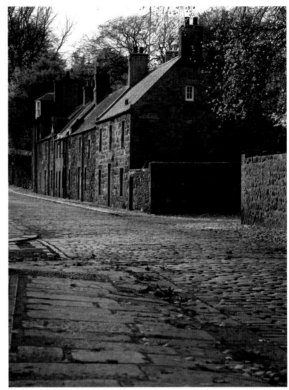

their charm lies in the absolute excellence and refinement of the details. The glazing bars of the windows are finely shaped and precisely tapered; the ironwork which guards the steps up to the front doors is invariably of the finest quality.

The garden of Humanity Manse is laid now to plain grass, and its western end is filled by modern halls of residence, still not quite at ease in their setting after almost half a century. Curiously, when the medieval requirement of residence in the college itself died out, the entire student body was lodged in widely variable degrees of comfort and discomfort in the private houses of Old Aberdeen and the Spital. It was only in the mid-twentieth century that student residences as such began once again to be built. Between the wars, interestingly, the students themselves were vocal in resistance to the creation of official university accommodation.

Passing down College Bounds, with a particularly agreeable group of modest Georgian houses on the left, two fantastical turrets soar up; their style might be identified as Saracenic with elements of Abbotsford Gothic. Forming, confusingly, the gate to a building itself known as Powis Gate, they are an answer of sorts to the pinnacles and tower of the college diagonally across the narrowing street. Through them lies an agreeable area of grass and trees with two modern halls of residence. One of them, Crombie Hall, built in the 1950s in the Scandinavian-modern style which is coming to look more and more at home in this northern city with the passage of time, has a wall of glass which reflects trees, villas and spires. Powis Gate is a freestanding house on the familiar manse-

Above. Powis Gate, formerly known as Powis House.

Right. Powis Lodge is now used as a nursery.

plan standing well back from the street. In the nineteenth century it was the home of a cultivated lawyer, and the university's art collection includes a fine double-portrait by Douglas Strachan of a music party in the drawing room, a painting intensely evocative of the secluded and elegant life of Old Aberdeen in the late nineteenth century. A second villa, Powis Lodge, is built behind an eighteenth-century cottage fronting the street. Its garden front is bay-windowed and picturesquely grouped, with a little turret to echo the gate-towers.

An overshadowed little path diving off to the left behind the last houses in College Bounds leads to the remains of the Snow Kirk, one of the most atmospheric and extraordinary places in all Scotland. All that remains, off the lane behind the back-garden fences, is the space once

Above. The Powis Burn (foreground) now flows underground, while football and cricket have replaced agricultural labour on the field behind King's. Oil painting by James Cassie, 1848, looking north-west from approximately where University Road meets Orchard Road today.

Opposite. New King's, west front, the High Street.

occupied by the church itself, the walls now standing only to shoulder-height. It is an extraordinary thought that Aberdonian tolerance and Aberdonian conservatism created a climate that allowed Catholic worship here to continue intermittently for a long time after the Reformation, and allowed of Catholic burials on this spot until the laws against the practice of Catholicism were at last repealed. It is a quiet, overlooked place, simple and moving: the great gravestone of the local Catholic magnate of the 'auld blood' of Aberdeen, Menzies of Pitfodels, lies at your feet; wall monuments record careers in that hidden and exiled Scotland enforced by the religious persecutions – Scalan and Valladolid, Regensburg and Rome; the graves of bishops of the penal times can no longer be traced. There are one or two more recent memorials to Catholic professors, and sometimes someone appears to lay flowers on a gravestone, but you are usually alone.

College Bounds has ended, merging into the High Street. Here one is in the heart of things, with crowds in the street in term time for five minutes either side of the hour, or moving in groups to the sports fields early on Wednesday afternoons. In vacations, especially in the depth of summer, the street can seem as quiet in the sunlight as if hayfields still stretched away for miles on every side, and the fall of water in a garden fountain opposite the college can be heard quite clearly. The wall on the right is the boundary of the ancient College Garden and, where it turns the corner into University Road, and still makes the edge of the original fortified college, although the stream which used to border it – Powis Burn – now runs to the sea through a culvert under the road. The two tall late-Georgian manses, with arched windows ingeniously fitted in between the flues of their chimney stacks, make handsome neighbours for the college itself. A glance to the left reveals the beautiful recession of the cobbled High Street to the north, articulated on the far side of generous lawns by the neo-Gothic stair-tower of the building (now a century old) called New King's, and by the subtle leftward curve of a continuous terrace of two-storey houses opposite. The polished stone and cupola-crowned pediment of the Old Town House closes the vista in the distance.

The façade of the college is dominated by the chapel tower, just as the founder intended: airy and massive at once, with the subtle tapering of its buttresses, leading the eye up the ribs that support the crown. The west end of the chapel is magnificent, especially when the doors are thrown open for the wedding of a former student or a university celebration, with the movement of tartan or black gowns against the mellow stone. At any time, one may see its stirring gilded inscription with King James IV's monogram and the record that the masons 'of this noble college' began the building in 1500, on 2 April, thereby marking the day and month

believed at the time to have been the commencement of the Temple of Solomon. There is so much to see: the flowing tracery of the windows, free and fluid to the point that comparison with art nouveau is not extravagant. The fine bronze monument to Bishop Elphinstone before the west door is a dignified twentieth-century reinvention of the original bronze monument, which was removed perhaps a century after the Reformation, or even later; Aberdonian caution and tolerance again in operation. The good bishop's actual grave lies within the chapel.

The college's central gate and front range are in a seemly and playful Regency Gothick, with pinnacles and beautifully detailed long windows on the first floor, lighting a delightful double-height room within. This was thoughtfully designed as a museum to house one of a series of displayed collections, the earliest firm record of which dates from 1751, making King's the site of Scotland's oldest continuous museum collection. The front range can be viewed to great advantage in the conditions so loved by Regency Romantic painters: after dark, on a night of full moon, its lit windows contrast with the bright, scudding clouds above.

The Victorian ranges within the quadrangle of the college are acquiring dignity with the passage of time, as are also the sculptured lion and unicorn which have elicited the affection of generations of students. The south wall of the chapel now provides a sheltered trap for the intermittent sun that illuminates the bright heraldry which delights the eye against the

Left. The Old Town House.

Opposite. The quadrangle at King's.

Elphinstone Lawn (above) was long covered by a manse in the style known as French Gothic, of which a single blurry image (opposite, left) appears to be the only visual record.

Opposite right. Sacrist, wedding guest and students in King's quad, seen from the porter's lodge.

sombre ashlar stonework in which they are set (the heraldry is described in Chapter Three, below). In the centre of the quadrangle is a well, a reminder that the college could shut its gates and put itself into a posture of defence, as it did when it successfully resisted a Calvinist mob from the Mearns in the early days of the Reformation. A university tradition, certainly in circulation by 1900 but probably much older, has this well as the dwelling of an eel of prodigious size and unimaginable antiquity, moving silently through the cold waters that lap at the foundations.

In the north-east corner of the quadrangle is the splendid (if much-altered) tower house that was built as a much-needed lodging range in the later 1650s. Tradition has named it Cromwell

Tower, but Oliver Cromwell had little if anything to do with it; the subscriptions that built it were raised among General George Monck's officers as well as local benefactors. It is now mostly given over to teaching rooms, with a few academic offices. From inside, it is appreciated ideally on a misty day, when the views out and down over the roofs of the chapel and into the dripping quadrangle take on a high-Victorian ghost-story quality.

A little passage between the east end of the chapel and the Cromwell Tower leads north towards the spacious Elphinstone Lawn, with its colonnade to the east. On or about St Cecilia's Day each year, the Aberdeen Musical Society assembles to perform instrumental music and songs drawn from the repertory of the old

Concert Club that flourished in Aberdeen in the second half of the eighteenth century. The fine painting of St Cecilia by the Jacobite painter Cosmo Alexander, which once belonged to the Musical Society, is now owned by the university but invariably makes a guest appearance on the evening of the concert. Passing the end of the chapel on a drizzling evening of early dark, one might hear a true tenor voice, accompanied by harpsichord and cello, singing one of the saddest songs of parting to have come out of the weary years of the Jacobite wars:

It's Lochaber no more and Lochaber no more,
I'll never return to Lochaber no more.

It is a moment of extraordinary intensity, one which only Old Aberdeen's confluence of history, collective interests, and current musical establishment could create.

The arcade along the east side of Elphinstone Lawn, built surprisingly late in the twentieth century, forms at its southern end the front of the rooms where novelist Eric Linklater's collection of Scottish Colourist paintings are displayed. At its northern end, one finds the way into Elphinstone Hall: the large ceremonial room of King's College, in which hang five enormous seventeenth-century canvases of Old Testament subjects, known as 'Black Paintings', which it is thought once ornamented the presence chamber of King Charles II when he was, in the early 1650s, prisoner-monarch of the Covenanters.

Looking west across the great expanse of

Elphinstone Lawn, the neat succession of two-storey houses along the High Street begins. The house opposite the chapel is a fine structure of the three-bay manse type, set unusually far back from the street. The deep front garden has recently been laid out in a wholly successful semi-formal style: the referents are the great English gardens of the mid-twentieth century – Hidcote, Sissinghurst – and the combination of clipped hedges, urns and informal herbaceous planting works just as well in the north as it does in the south.

Heading north up the High Street to the Old Town House, the cobbled street narrows between taller and more varied buildings. On the right is a particularly handsome three-bay house, unusually tall, with semicircular bay windows on either side of the door. Also on the right, up Grant's Place, one can find the confident and beautiful memorial to the MacRobert family, extraordinary and tragic benefactors to the university. A coloured mosaic with their arms takes up the whole of the far wall, and an armillary sundial is reflected in a still pool: there are seats and shelter from the wind, quiet, and barely a ripple on the surface of the water.

These narrows of the High Street in rainy winter dusk, with the cobbles glistening a little treacherously underfoot, easily feel as though they are slipping in time. The crowds of students leaving their last classes of the day can seem like the whole population of the early-modern burgh hurrying through the street towards the cross in front of the Town House at some past crisis of war, rumour or proclamation. On the left, set well back from the street is the town house of the MacLeans of Coll, a building of adroitly under-stated grandeur, its middle bay advanced a little with the central window breaking the line of the pediment, the whole ensemble framed by the piers of the carriage gates with foot gates to either side.

Here the High Street opens out to form a triangular marketplace in front of the tall, iconic, and finely pedimented Old Town House, with

the remains of the burgh's Market Cross in the middle of the cobbles before it. There are some magnificent houses to the left, with fine, cut-ashlar fronts. In a surprisingly humble house to the right lived the natural philosopher William MacGillivray, who was the collaborator with J.J. Audubon in the mighty enterprise of producing the illustrated volumes of the *Birds of America*: one of the greatest achievements in the history of the illustrated book.

The dignified Old Town House has recently been the subject of a carefully considered restoration by the university. On the ground floor, opposite two former police cells now used for storage, is the reception for visitors, which features an architect's model of the new university library. An audacious and beautiful building of glass, very much a building of the North, the library will soon become the early twenty-first century's most notable adornment to the burgh. On the first floor, in a spacious room whose mirroring fireplaces, dado-panelling and

considered proportions are a reminder of the depth of the northern Scots connection with Scandinavia and the Baltic, continuously maintained exhibitions of contemporary art are freely open to the public. In the dignified and more ornate double-height meeting room on the top floor – used in bygone days as a masonic lodge – there are revolving exhibitions of the university's ancient pictures: the bishops of Aberdeen who adorned the Common Hall of King's; the nostalgic series of Stuart monarchs who hung in the Common Hall at Marischal.

From the tall windows, looking south down the length of the High Street to where it tapers to its vanishing point at the beginning of College Bounds, you are confronted by one of the most satisfying, and memorable, urban views in Scotland: the shape of the marketplace, the quality of detailing on the buildings, the varying degrees of reflected light from polished ashlar, cobble and freestone.

The street anciently divided into two at the

Left. Elphinstone Hall was designed by A. Marshall Mackenzie and completed in 1931.

Right. The High Street, looking north and west from King's College Chapel.

Town House: one branch led into the seclusion of the Chanonry and ended at the cathedral in front of the plantations of the Seaton estate; the other, now called Don Street, was the continuation of the highway to the north, which was once the only road to Balgownie and its all-important river crossing. The needs of the modern city have led a relief road, St Machar Drive, along the back of the Town House over what was once the extensive garden and painted gallery of the Gordons of Cluny. Crossing this, if one takes the right-hand fork, Don Street is curving and densely built, a combination of two-storey houses and cottages with slightly incongruous nineteenth-century tenements; the strongly vertical Bishop's Gate is a seventeenth-century burgh house of pleasing design with its little stair-turret corbelled out in the angle between wings. Standing back from the street, with ample gardens to the front, is another of the handsome houses of the manse type, this one the dower house for Grandhome, a country house just outside the city on the other side of the river. At the bottom of Don Street the ancient burgh fades out into pleasant and modest twentieth-century housing. A silent lane, its paving alternately cobble and flagstone, leads between garden walls to the villas in gardens and plain granite cottages of Dunbar Street, once the Back Dykes of Don Street.

Up to the left is the house called the Chaplain's Court, whose exposed masonry

Opposite top. Wright's and Cooper's Place at night.

Opposite bottom. The High Street house built by the MacLeans of Coll.

Right. Spontaneous scilla.

offers a beguiling jigsaw puzzle, constituting in itself a history of Scottish building over many centuries. Over the entrance to a filled-in archway are the arms of Bishop Gavin Dunbar (d. 1532). The rest of the house is a long three-storey block, with a secluded garden. Next to it stands the cathedral manse and further up are stone gate-piers with a vacant lot behind. For a moment the illusion is powerful that this is still the lost city of Gordon's or Roy's maps and that there is nothing beyond but the policies of Seaton House, the links and the sea.

The Chanonry proper is best approached by a return to the Town House, and crossing the main road by its left-hand side. On the corner is the university's botany department, facing the little brick-and-stone wing that is all that remains of the house of Gordon of Cluny. Almost as soon as you turn into the Chanonry, the garden walls, cobbles and overhanging trees, as well as the disposition of the houses echo the seclusion and enclosure of the cathedral close that it once was.

To the right is a regular row of the late-

Opposite top. Inside the Town House: exhibitions ancient and modern.

Opposite bottom. The view south, down High Street from the Old Town House.

Below. The Chanonry.

23

Cluny's Port, displaying Old Aberdeen's characteristic granite-and-red-brick construction.

eighteenth-century manse-type houses, grander and more spacious than most of the houses in the High Street. (It is an agreeable puzzle to spot which of them is an accomplished neo-Georgian pastiche.) This delightful row gives way to the immense length of the garden wall of the Chanonry Lodge.

On the other side of the street are the open gates of the Cruickshank Botanic Gardens, one of the delights and secrets of Old Aberdeen: a delight because of the endless horticultural skill which keeps a succession of flowering plants informally disposed about the grounds; a secret because the street lines conceal both the sheer extent of the garden, and its variety. Beyond this are two exemplary large town houses, one with the verticality and square third-floor windows of

the earlier eighteenth century, the second a perfectly tuned variation on the pedimented three-bay design with a sweep of steps up to the front door. The line is broken by the three-sided courtyard of the Mitchell Hospital, a classic almshouse plan with a bellcote breaking the skyline. Beyond is a small Regency country house in the city, Tillydrone House, standing well back from the road in what is in effect a miniature landscaped park. Ahead is St Machar's Cathedral in its dense, stony churchyard, with charming bowed gatehouses in the same Regency Gothick as the west front of the college. The cathedral's own west front is a magnificent reminder of the long and strong links between northern Scotland and the northlands of Scandinavia: sheer, plain, with two monumental

buttressed towers with stone spires.

Facing the cathedral is the house which was long the most important building in the lost city. From their town palace at 13 The Chanonry, now known as Chanonry Lodge, the Great Gordons, marquises and earls of Huntly – viceroys, if you like – once ruled as if Aberdeenshire and Moray were a principality, independent from the rest of Scotland. Fittingly, Chanonry Lodge now serves as the residence of the university principal.

The tall gate piers at its entrance give way to a *cour d'honneur*, the *corps de logis* ahead, wings reaching forward on either side. Imagine a summer reception with the door in its pedimented surround standing open, revealing the polished wood of the hall with its fine paintings, then the great drawing room, and then the panelled dining room, its walls hung with dashing, melancholy portraits of Jacobite captains of the 1715 rising. Stretching the length of the back of the house is a wonderful conservatory or orangery; again the feeling of the modest splendour of northern Europe is strong. It is easy to imagine the scent of citrus blossom within and snow outside, or plants in tubs set out on the spacious terrace as they would be on a summer evening. Look around at the sheer scale of the garden, its mature trees, the slanting sunbeams on smooth lawn, the smaller, yet still massive, houses just visible through the leaves beyond the brick garden walls. The scale is remarkable. This is indeed a vice-regal or ducal palace, fit for the governor of Scotland's lost city.

CHAPTER TWO

From the Beginning

Aberdeen has been a place of some importance since there were any people in Scotland at all. The earliest monument to human presence, Long Cairn, is between 4,000 and 6,000 years old. At least three stone circles testify to the importance it held for the early inhabitants of the region. Compared with Scotland's western seaboard, fissured with inlets like a miniature version of Norway, the east coast is relatively bleak and bare: north of the River Don, much of the coast

Opposite. The mighty River Don in spate.

Bird Life

One group of local inhabitants it is impossible to overlook are the herring gulls. They waddle to and fro among the hurrying students, indifferent to human presence. Large birds, with sharp and formidable beaks, they are perfectly well aware that they have little to worry about. There is one Aberdonian bird which has achieved international internet notoriety due to its passion for cheese Doritos, but in general, gulls will eat most things. Although one would normally think of them as fish-eaters, their liking for worms gives rise to a characteristic and comic pattern of behaviour: after a rainy night, a bird standing gloomily on the lawn will suddenly go into what seems to be a dance routine, its pink feet twinkling as it jigs on the spot. But this is not entertainment; worms are attracted by the vibration and the gull is keeping a close eye on the ground. When an unwary worm pokes its head up, it is whipped out of its burrow by the gull's sharp beak.

While herring gulls mooch and scavenge all over Scotland's coastal cities, Old Aberdeen plays host to some less-expected residents. Oystercatchers, fast and highly acrobatic black-and-white birds with long red beaks, normally stay close to the shoreline, but they are surprisingly often seen zooming across the burgh uttering the wild piping cries which make them sound as if they are in a perpetual state of over-excitement or competing for worms with the herring gulls. This is because some years ago, they colonised the flat gravel-covered roofs of an office building in Regent Walk. To the eye of an oystercatcher, the roofs were safe and secluded shingle beaches where they could raise their chicks without fear of disturbance. When the university began a round of repairing and consolidating the roofs, which involved replacing the gravel with a rubber

coating, plastic seed-trays full of pebbles were set out for the oystercatchers, who accepted these nesting boxes quite unperturbed. Since the birds can live for twenty years, and generations of chicks have been successfully reared, they are probably now to be deemed permanent residents. Old Aberdeen has the highest population of urban oystercatchers anywhere in Europe.

Other birds worth looking out for, in winter, are waxwings. These are exotics from Siberia and Scandinavia who migrate in large flocks. They are regular visitors to the group of rowan trees on University Road by the tennis court. They are tiny, pretty creatures with pink and charcoal feathers, and since they have very little natural fear of man, it is possible to admire them from close quarters as they cavort in the branches, pecking at berries.

From the fifteenth-century Hortus Sanitatis, *annotated by Aberdeen apothecary George Peacock.*

is beaches and sand dunes; south of the River Dee there are many miles of cliffs. Both major rivers, the Don and the Dee run to the sea within two miles of one another, and their estuaries offered a relatively easy way of life to Stone Age man. Even with primitive log boats, salmon could be taken in wicker fish-traps, or speared; the shoreline offered shellfish, and seabirds (see box, p.27) and their eggs. Between the mouths of the two rivers, sand and gravel deposited at the end of the last Ice Age made a series of mounds running roughly north–south, where huts could be built on dry, firm ground, but at no great distance from fresh water and abundant food supplies.

Earliest Times

It is clear from archaeological records that both settlement, and the ritual activity witnessed by circles and standing stones, occurred around both rivers, with no apparent preference for one or the other. But by the time Aberdeen emerges from obscurity to the point of acquiring a name, the settlement on the Dee was more important. In the second century AD, the Greek geographer Ptolemy, who was surprisingly well informed about the British Isles, wrote of a place called Devana, the only 'polis' – which might mean township or trading settlement – belonging to a tribe called the Taexali. How did he know? Probably from military intelligence, since in the summer of AD 84, the Roman general Agricola took an army far into the north of Scotland. A chain of Roman temporary marching camps is strung along the foothills of the Grampians from the Montrose area up as far as Spey Bay, including one just south of New Aberdeen.

'Deva', which later became Dee, is a well-attested Celtic river name, shared with the River Dee of Wales, and perhaps the Deva of northern Spain. 'Don' is also a very ancient river name, used by British Celts, since it is shared with the Dons of Lancashire and South Yorkshire as well as with the mighty Don which flows through Russia. The name Aberdeen combines the Celtic word *aber* (place where a river flows into the sea) with either 'Don', or *da-abhuin* (of two rivers). Nomenclature therefore suggests that by the end of the first century, the people who had settled between the river mouths were Celtic speakers.

Though the name of the town may suggest the primacy of the Don, it was the settlement on the Dee which developed as a trading site, having a much better harbourage. But the hilly area overlooking the Don was not entirely neglected. The plentiful salmon of the Don fishing were as tempting as they had ever been, and will not have gone unexploited. There is also actual evidence of human habitation in the early second century, at the site now known as Tillydrone Motte (see box opposite). Its name is Celtic, *tulach draighinn*, 'the hill of thorns'.

The first name associated with Old Aberdeen is that of St Machar. According to legend, he was a companion of the sixth-century missionary saint, Columba of Iona, though no one of that name appears in the near-contemporary *Life of Columba* by Adomnán of Iona. Whenever it started, the legend of St Machar was fully developed by the fourteenth century, when an anonymous Scot turned it into verse. This is supported by two other versions, both from the sixteenth century: one by an Irish scholar, Manus O'Donnell, and one in the Breviary of Aberdeen. All three agree that Machar was an Irishman of good family, educated by St Columba (who renamed him *Macarius*, 'blessèd'). Machar became the saint's favourite disciple but his extreme holiness caused so much jealousy and bad feeling – even an attempted poisoning – that Columba sadly suggested it would be better for everyone if he went elsewhere to preach the gospel. Columba, who was gifted with second sight, told Machar that he would know the place where God intended him to settle when he found a stream shaped like a bishop's crozier. After various adventures, he came to the lower reaches of the Don, where he stood on high ground looking down at the U-shaped loop made by the river, and saw in it his Promised Land. (It is often said that this cannot be right since early Celtic croziers were simple wooden staffs, but the representations of St Matthew as a bishop with a crozier in the Mac Durnan Gospels and the crozier-carrying ecclesiastic on the Round Tower of Brechin both have staffs sharply curved at the top like an old-fashioned walking stick – or, indeed, like the surviving crozier of St Fillan). There, Machar, 'by the efficacy of his prayer . . .

turned into stone a savage monster which was wont to devastate that region, and slay all it met with its poisonous breath and belching'. He also built a church, and converted the local inhabitants to Christianity.

Eventually, the legend continues, Machar was appointed by Pope Gregory the Great to the see of Tours, the most important church in France, where he served for three and a half years before being summoned to heaven. It is probably needless to add that the succession of sixth-century bishops of Tours is well attested, and none of them can conceivably be identified with St Machar. The most surprising thing about this story is that the whereabouts of the saint's body is left unclear. Given the importance of pilgrimage to ecclesiastical revenue and to medieval life in general, one would really have expected the angels to deliver Machar's remains back to the church at Old Aberdeen. That they did not suggests the entire narrative is fantastical.

Whatever the truth – or lack of it – of this story, the episcopal see of Old Aberdeen is a

From Hortus Sanitatis.

Tillydrone Motte: A Glimpse into Old Aberdeen's Earliest History

The artificial hill known as Tillydrone Motte, now at the south end of Seaton Park, recently revealed its secrets. A 'motte' is a type of medieval fortification introduced to Scotland by the Normans. Several survive from the twelfth century onwards. In the nineteenth century, the romantically minded accounted for the mound in Seaton Park by a picturesque legend: the nuns of St Katherine's in the Chanonry had created it as a penance, carrying up the earth from the low ground of Seaton in their aprons. Less fanciful souls

assumed that it was a motte, and only a moderately impressive example of the type. But the erosion of several tracks down the side of the mound gave a reason for scheduling excavations in 2001–02. This work sprung several surprises, the biggest of which was that it was not a medieval site at all. At the heart of the mound there was a sizeable stone structure which seems to have been a cairn, a site of elaborate burials in the Bronze Age. This cairn was then reused hundreds of years later, in the second century AD, and the

top was fenced off to make a defensive stockade, presumably surrounding a group of buildings. On the south-east of the mound there was an entrance which allowed access to this modest fort through a gate. A fragment of 'Samian ware' pottery in the region of a hearth, which can only have come from trading with the Romans, suggests that these people's lives were touched, however distantly, by a wider world. They are the first known inhabitants of Old Aberdeen.

mystery that needs explaining. By the early twelfth century, the thriving and growing community of fishermen and merchants at the mouth of the Dee was big enough and important enough to be given the status of a royal burgh, and to be visited in person by the active and talented King David I. A major church was built there, dedicated to St Nicholas, a saint of Christendom in general with no local association. The Don was not capable of supporting a parallel development. Hector Boece (c.1465–1536), historian and first principal of Aberdeen University, stated that the bishopric of Aberdeen was founded at Mortlach around 1010, and not transferred to Aberdeen until 1136.

Mortlach was an important place in the early middle ages. A bull of Pope Adrian IV's, written in 1157, refers to 'the township and monastery of Mortlach with five [dependent] churches and the lands thereunto pertaining', so it was clearly the centre of church organisation for a significant part of Banff. The abbot of Mortlach quite probably was a bishop, common practice in the Irish and Scoto-Irish church. The one thing that is certain is that by the thirteenth century there was a stone church, dedicated to the otherwise obscure St Machar, perched on a bluff above the Don. Molua, who was associated with Mortlach, is never mentioned in association with Aberdeen. But if the rights and privileges of Mortlach were transferred, why was Molua forgotten, and why was the episcopal church of Aberdeen sited in the relatively undeveloped lands above the Don and not in the new royal burgh on the Dee?

The simplest answer to both questions is that

Mitchell Hospital.

there was indeed an individual, whose name was subsequently remembered as Mochonna and Latinised as Macarius, who had flourished in the early Middle Ages, and left a powerful reputation for holiness and a well-remembered site where his saintly days had been spent. The bishop's seat was consequently located on this holy ground. Alternatively, Professor Colm Ó Baoill has suggested that 'St Machar' is in fact St Mungo, or Kentigern, the patron saint of Glasgow, since there is ancient evidence of a cult of St Mungo on Deeside at Glengairn. He suggests that the name 'Machar' came about in the early part of the twelfth century when Gaelic was being replaced by Latin in and around Aberdeen, and the story was developed subsequently.

Thus, rather than developing concentrically from a single centre, the Aberdeen of the mid-twelfth century was shaped like a dumbbell. The commercial centre was, and would always remain, the settlement on the Dee in the south. But the religious centre was the settlement on the Don. Between them was the bar of the dumbbell: a firm, raised ridge, two miles long, later called Spitalhill after St Peter's Hospital, one of the area's several almshouses (see box, p.32), a refuge for 'infirm brethren'. Standing proud of the marshy ground between the two river mouths, Spitalhill ensured that transit between one centre and the other was fairly straightforward, regardless of the time of year.

Thus, paradoxically, 'New Aberdeen' is older than 'Old Aberdeen', certainly in terms of its legal status, since New Aberdeen was a royal burgh by 1153 at the latest, and Old Aberdeen did not acquire independent burghal status until 1489. Old Aberdeen's first inhabitants, apart from fishermen, were presumably the men who built (and, as we will see, continually rebuilt) St

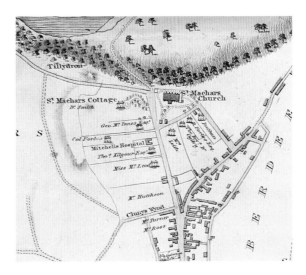

Machar's, the men who served the cathedral, and those who depended on them.

Cathedral City

The Celtic Church was unusual, the organic product of cityless regions with very little in the way of centralised organisation. The centres of Celtic Christianity were not cathedrals, but monasteries. Monasteries are naturally centres for prayer and contemplation, but not for ministry. Instruction of laypeople, education, and the provision of sacraments such as baptism, marriage and burial were certainly undertaken, but not always in an orderly and organised fashion, or consistently.

In the course of the twelfth century, as the Celtic lands came more and more under Norman influence, this began to seem inadequate. In Ireland, St Malachy undertook the reform of the church; in Scotland, this task fell to King David. Having spent a great deal of his early life at the court of his brother-in-law, Henry I of England, David was greatly impressed with Anglo-

Almshouses

Almshouses have been a marked feature of the Old Aberdeen townscape, and one of them, the Mitchell Hospital, is still to be seen. The earliest known almshouse was the leper hospital which gave the Spital its name, just south of Old Aberdeen proper. Leprosy, or Hansen's Disease as it is now named, is not very contagious as infectious diseases go, but it was, and is, terrifying because of the gross and incurable disfigurement it inflicts. In the small, insanitary and overcrowded dwellings of the Middle Ages, beds, plates and cups were shared, and in winter people lived huddled together for warmth; the disease easily made its way from one to another. At least one of Scotland's kings, Robert the Bruce, is now believed to have died from the disease. In the absence of any cure, the only answer was to segregate those who fell victim and so leper hospitals arose at a safe distance from centres of population everywhere in medieval Europe.

The colony on the Spital existed by 1363, and was still operating in 1604, when the kirk session declared that 'a puir woman infectit with Leprosie . . . be put into the Hospitall appoyntit for keiping and haulding of Lipper folkis betwix the townis and the keyis of the said hospital to be deliverit to hir'. Helen Smyth was her name. Though the disease was far less of a problem in the Europe of the 1600s than it had been in earlier centuries, it lingered longest in the North where hard winters kept the inhabitants living cheek by jowl. At least five lepers entered the house in the Spital between 1591 and 1612.

The lepers were supported by charity: they were permitted to beg, but beyond that, a croft was farmed on their behalf by a tenant of the town council. The support provided by the croft may have been inadequate, since according to a 1591 charter of James VI, 'they leif verie miserablie, specialie in the Wynter time.' This may be because the unfortunate lepers, whose capacity to act on their own behalf was limited by their seclusion, were cheated of their dues. James Leslie, who rented the croft in the 1570s, failed to pay his rent for five years, during which time food and fuel must have been in short supply in the leper house.

The last known leper was Agnes Jameson, who entered the house in 1612. By the time Parson Gordon drew his map of the two Aberdeens in 1661, the Spital leper house appears merely as 'ruins of the Sick house', and in 1715, the croft which supported it was sold by the town, the money raised being devoted to charitable ends.

Bishop Dunbar endowed another almshouse in 1532. The building was swept away in the eighteenth century, but it stood near the west end of St Machar's, just north of where the Tillydrone Road springs from the Chanonry, in what is now Seaton Park, and was

Horn and silver beakers from Mitchell Hospital, dated 1801.

intended to accommodate twelve poor elderly men. In the prologue of its charter, Dunbar stated that 'whatever was left from the fruits of his church to any prelate, after satisfying the necessities of the church and his own life, the prelate is bound to devote to the poor and disadvantaged'. His regulations laid out the building he envisaged with great precision. It was to be 100 feet long and 32 feet wide, with twelve rooms 14 feet by 12 feet. There was a common room on the north side, 16 feet by 36 feet, with a fire, storage space for fuel above it, and a double-height oratory on the south side. The building had a central steeple, resembling that of King's but built of timber, which housed a bell.

The old men who lived there had yearly pensions of ten merks (£6 13s 4d) to buy what they needed for themselves, and another merk to buy a white surcoat which they wore as a distinctive uniform. They were also encouraged to contribute to their own support by working in the garden. But above all, they were bedesmen – their principal job was to pray for the health and soul of the king, and for the souls of their benefactors. At least three hours a day were to be spent in prayer.

Despite the founder's emphasis on the saying and hearing of mass, the old bedehouse survived the Reformation because, as an old-age home, it was so obviously doing useful work for the town. It remained on the site until 1786, when James Forbes of Seaton exchanged a house in Don Street, subsequently called the Bede House, for the old building. Presumably Forbes demolished the old edifice in order to landscape the grounds of Seaton House. It is not at all clear whether any bedesmen actually lived communally in the new Bede House, but the endowments survived under the name of the Bede Fund, and did continue to be used to support the elderly. As late as 1929, Local historian Katherine Trail noted that eighteen old

men from the parish received 12s a month (useful money in 1929), and an annual salmon. They were the last royal bedesmen in Scotland, still required to pray daily for the king's soul, and when Queen Mary visited St Machar's in the 1920s, they were drawn up outside the cathedral door to welcome her. There are no longer bedesmen in Old Aberdeen, but the Bede House sheltered housing complex on St Machar Drive is the effective descendant of Bishop Dunbar's foundation, which has given the modern development its name.

A corresponding foundation for women, the Mitchell Hospital, is still standing. Old Aberdeen was always rather well provided with elderly women, and those who became too old and frail to care for themselves were obviously a problem since they were not eligible to join Bishop Dunbar's foundation. The United Trades of Old Aberdeen therefore decided to endow a suitable home for women at the beginning of the eighteenth century. They owned some land in the Chanonry, and in 1711 they built a hospital there. The endowment was meagre; in 1765 the trustees were irritated to find that the widows and spinsters they supported preferred to take the little pension which came with the accommodation and find their own homes – probably because a room in a family house was warmer. The trustees decreed that they would not pay the endowment to anyone who did not live in the hospital, 'it being to the loss of the house greatly to want possessors, who must burn fire therein'. This suggests that the house was becoming run down, and therefore harder to heat, and in 1792 it was sold for £50 sterling.

The problem, of course, did not go away. Nearly ten years later, in 1801, David Mitchell, a native of Old Aberdeen who had spent his life in Essex, created a new and improved foundation to answer the same purposes as the earlier Trades Hospital. Mitchell's hospital was built to accommodate five widows and five unmarried

daughters of trade and merchant burgesses of Old Aberdeen, and in his detailed instructions for the inmates' way of life, Mitchell clearly envisaged a sort of secular convent. The women were to dress uniformly, in dark blue, and to live communally: each had her own room where she could make her own breakfast and tea, but there were no private cooking facilities. Dinner was a communal meal served in a refectory. The women were to take turns to cook, and their menu was laid down: they were allowed beef three times a week as long as it was less than 4d a pound, but if it got more expensive than that, they could only have it twice. Otherwise, the main course was to be fish or eggs. Mitchell added, 'as it is impossible to keep order and regularity among ten women except one of them have a superiority over the rest, I appoint the trustees to choose a sensible, discreet woman to be the Governess or Mistress.' Those who were capable of a little work were allowed to keep half of what they earned so that they could buy snuff or tobacco.

Mitchell Hospital was better endowed than the previous Trades Hospital, and far more successful. But in the twentieth century the trustees found themselves facing the same problem as other almshouse trusts: how to maintain the usefulness of a visually charming and distinctive structure while answering twentieth-century expectations of private kitchens and bathrooms. In 1924, the whole building was imaginatively remodelled by the architect A.H.L. Mackinnon (1870–1937), who kept the façade intact. He turned it into four self-contained houses, each consisting of living room, two bedrooms, bathroom, kitchenette, and larder, unified by a landscaped garden. It continues as a visual reminder of an older, more communal way of life in Scotland, and a precious survival of a type of building that has proved very vulnerable to changing patterns of life.

Right. St Machar's Cathedral from the north-west in 1842. Use of the kilt at this time and place is questionable, and may have sprung from the fancy of the painter John Moir, who was born in Peterhead, Aberdeenshire.

Opposite. Bishop Gavin Dunbar (d. 1532).

Norman ways. He would give the nation its first silver coinage and launch an ambitious programme of urban development. The foundation of Aberdeen, in particular, was part of a more general attempt on his part to create a new kind of regularity and order in the Scottish church. According to Ailred of Rievaulx, a reform-minded Anglo-Norman abbot who greatly admired David, he found three or four bishops in the whole Scottish kingdom (north of the Forth), and the others wavering without a pastor, to the loss of both morals and property. When he died he left nine bishoprics, both ancient ones which he himself had restored and new ones which he had erected.

At Brechin, Dunblane and Dunkeld, bishops who had been (in the old Celtic fashion) the heads of monastic houses rather than episcopal sees, were made part of a national diocesan system. A bishopric of Caithness was created, and the rights and privileges of the monastery at Mortlach were transferred to Aberdeen.

According to Hector Boece, the cathedral church of St Machar's in Old Aberdeen was begun in 1165, about thirty-five years later than the beginning assigned to it in the probably fictive account in the Bishops' Register. There is an identifiable Scottish–Norman style of church, like the twelfth-century churches which survive at Monymusk and Leuchars: a simple and unpretentious stone building with massively thick walls, windows arched at the top, and perhaps a semicircular apse at the east end, the end with the altar table in it. It is a fair guess that the first cathedral was a building of this kind.

Nechtan, first bishop of Aberdeen, bore an ancient Pictish name, but the task given him by the king was one of modernisation. In the course of the thirteenth century, the clerics who served St Machar's discovered the apparently universal truth that reform of any kind involves an exponential increase in paperwork. The price of having an organised, national church was that it must actually become organised. Nechtan's church had been built for worship, but the proliferation of business meant that a committee room was needed too and there was nowhere suitable. By the middle of the thirteenth century, when there were thirteen canons living in the Chanonry engaged on cathedral business, they needed not only a committee room, but a library – containing reference books to deal with the more complex problems that might come their way – and a court. In the medieval world, much of what would now be thought of as family law was the province of church courts, as were a variety of issues of faith, morals, and clerical behaviour.

Thus another of Aberdeen's great bishops, Henry Cheyne (d. 1328), decided in the 1280s that a much more elaborate set of buildings was necessary. The daily service of the mass and preaching could on no account be suspended, so he screened off the nave, where the people stood, as an interim church, and behind a temporary curtain-wall he began to extend the simple, hemispherical apse of Bishop Nechtan's church into the three short arms of a great cross.

Two massive pillars survive from Cheyne's

plan. When Edward I invaded Scotland, Cheyne was forced to swear fealty to him, and when Robert the Bruce regained control, the bishop was exiled. He was accordingly unable to continue with his ambitious scheme (though some stories suggest that the beneficiary was another of his unfinished projects, the Brig o' Balgownie). Cheyne's successors continued to demonstrate their interest and pride in their church by beautifying and elaborating it. When Alexander Kininmund became bishop in 1355, he returned to the cathedral building-site, and took matters in hand. In the twenty-five years of his episcopate, Kininmund built the huge cylindrical pillars which are a strong feature of the interior to this day. He also began remaking the outer walls, and created one of Old Aberdeen's strongest visual icons, second only to the crowned spire of King's College, by building the two vast, squat towers at the west end.

The beginning of the fifteenth century was a difficult period in Scotland: the legitimate king, James I, was a captive in England from age ten to twenty-eight, and did not manage to regain his position until 1424. James's return brought a measure of peace and order, and this was reflected in St Machar's by renewed building, instigated by Bishop Henry Lychton. He completed the nave and aisles, and the west front, between Kininmund's twin towers. Ingram Lindsay attended to the fine details of the great stone shell created by his predecessor Lychton. He roofed the nave, paved the floor, glazed the windows, and decorated the walls throughout the 1440s and 1450s. William Elphinstone completed the chancel by adding a belfry and spire to the central tower – and for the first time, we can name a builder, John Fendour. The spire was covered in lead, as was the roof. Also probably dating to this period is the cathedral's miraculous statue, known as 'Our Lady of Aberdeen'. This was already culted in the time of Elphinstone's immediate successor as bishop, Gavin Dunbar, for when he completed Elphinstone's bridge over the Dee, he moved it to a little chapel built for the purpose on the bridge's first arch. Late in his episcopate Dunbar changed his mind and brought her back, and in St Machar's she remained until the Reformation. Dunbar also added the spires to Kininmund's towers and created the glorious heraldic ceiling (see box, p.38) which still, amazingly, survives. In the first 400 years of the cathedral's existence, there can have been few decades where there was no work in progress at St Machar's. As with the more famous cathedrals of France, it was a truly multi-generational labour of love.

Scotland's first national poet, John Barbour, was archdeacon of St Machar's Cathedral for forty years. Since the manse built and supported by the people of the diocese of Old Rayne, 11 The Chanonry, was designated for the use of the archdeacon, that is presumably where Barbour lived. Most of the cathedral canons must have spent their working lives oscillating within a tiny orbit of less than a hundred yards between their manses and the cathedral, but not the archdeacon, who spent much of his working life on horseback, quartering the hills and fields of the diocese, which covered both modern Aberdeenshire and Buchan. His studies had taken him to both Oxford and Paris, so he was a man of wide human experience as well as considerable learning.

His epic romance, *The Brus*, was written in Old Aberdeen in 1375, when he was sixty. It earned him a royal gift of £10 Scots and a life pension of twenty shillings per annum which,

like a true son of the middle ages, he elected to spend on an annual mass for the souls of himself and his parents.

Like the *Scotichronicon*, written by Barbour's contemporary and probable Chanonry neighbour, John of Fordun (see box below), Barbour's poem on Robert the Bruce is truly a national work. It tells the story of the Bruce's great victory over the English at the battle of Bannockburn, near Stirling: one of the key moments in Scottish history, since the loss of that battle would have meant the loss of Scottish independence. At the beginning of the fourteenth century the powerful and aggressive Edward I attempted, with considerable success, to annex the smaller and poorer kingdom to his north. Scottish opposition was fierce, led, above all, by William Wallace, who was executed in London in 1305. Edward himself died in 1307, on his way to crush a new rebellion in Scotland, led by Robert the Bruce. Edward was succeeded by his son, Edward II, who, as soon as he had set

Opposite. St Machar's Cathedral from the south gate.

John of Fordun

John of Fordun was the principal author of a history of Scotland known as the *Scotichronicon*, begun towards the end of the fourteenth century. In the prologue to the manuscript copy of his work known as *The Black Book of Paisley*, now in the British Library, he is called *capellanus ecclesie Aberdonensis* (a chaplain of the church of Aberdeen), so, like his contemporary John Barbour, he was one of the clergy of St Machar's and probably a resident of the Chanonry. His work was scrupulously researched. Very little had been written about the history of Scotland before his time, but what there was he read, suggesting that the cathedral library was well stocked. He also travelled in search of books; Walter Bower (1385–1449), who continued the work after Fordun laid down his pen, describes him as 'like an industrious bee', journeying endlessly from one university or monastic library to another, searching for annals and other historical documents. Their *Scotichronicon* is the basic document for medieval Scottish history. It was greatly valued by Hector Boece, who presented a fine copy to Aberdeen University; for some unknown reason, this copy passed into private ownership in the seventeenth century, and is now in Trinity College, Cambridge.

The Heraldic Ceiling of St Machar's

Only two completely intact medieval wooden ceilings survive in Scottish churches, both of which are in Old Aberdeen. The ceiling of King's College Chapel is one, and the ceiling of the nave of St Machar's Cathedral (pictured opposite) is the other. The cathedral's ceiling is dateable, for Hector Boece was preparing his lives of the bishops of Aberdeen for publication in 1520–21, and observed that as he was writing the ceiling was almost complete. It was a major undertaking, probably over two or more years. Thomas Orem, in his early eighteenth-century history of the Chanonry, recorded the local tradition that the craftsman who made the ceiling was called James Winter, and came from Angus.

It is less easy to name the individual who designed the cathedral ceiling, but the strongest candidate is Alexander Galloway (d. 1552), rector of Kinkell and architect. Galloway designed both the Brig o' Dee and Greyfriars Church in the New Town. One unusual feature of the ceiling is that it is flat. When medieval Scottish churches were given wooden ceilings, these were normally of a shape that resembled stone vaulting. The second arresting feature of the ceiling is its scheme of decoration, which is unique in Europe. Normally a church was decorated with scenes from the Holy Scriptures or from the legends of the saints, so that even the illiterate might gain some knowledge of Christian teaching. However, the person who designed the ceiling of St Machar's set out to educate the citizens of Aberdeen on the politics of the time. While it was under construction, the Lutheran revolt in Germany was in the process of destroying the traditional concept of Europe as a united spiritual and political entity. The ceiling records that traditional unity at the moment when it was about to disappear forever.

It is decorated with forty-eight shields, arranged in three series of sixteen coats of arms, running its whole length from east to west. The series of shields on the central axis of the ceiling, in the place of honour, are those of the Holy Church itself. The Pope is also represented. In 1520, the office was held by Giovanni de' Medici of Florence, who bore the papal name of Leo X, so it is his arms that are depicted. Within the space of a few months, precisely at the time when the St Machar's ceiling was being created, Pope Leo excommunicated Martin Luther and, ironically, conferred the title of 'Defender of the Faith' on King Henry VIII. Following on from the papal coat of arms are the arms of the archbishops of St Andrews and of Glasgow; those of the other eleven territorial bishops of the Scottish Church; the prior of St Andrews, which was then the most important religious house in the kingdom; and finally, those of King's College.

The line of shields along the south side of the ceiling, heraldically the 'dexter' or more important side, depicts the coats of arms of the king of Scots and the nobility of Scotland, ending with those of New Aberdeen. Along the north side of the nave, the heraldic 'sinister' side, lesser in importance and dignity, we have the coats of arms of the Holy Roman Emperor (Charles V) and the kings of Christendom: France, in honour of the 'Auld Alliance', followed by Spain, then England, and finally Old Aberdeen itself. Thus it is both a statement about 'the Christian nations under God', and of national and local pride. Having survived all tempests, religious, political and meteorological, it was restored in 1869–71.

matters in order at home, led a campaign to Scotland with the intention of completing his father's project and crushing Scottish insurgency once and for all. He marched north with an army of 40,000, enormous by medieval standards, and met the Bruce in the environs of Stirling. In defiance of expectations – on either side – English pretensions to rule Scotland were annihilated by the far smaller Scottish army. Bannockburn was fought in June 1314, around the time of Barbour's birth; he would grow up in a world shaped by this battle and its aftermath.

The delighted King Robert II who awarded him his pension was the Bruce's grandson.

What Barbour wrote was a poem aimed at defining Scottish nationhood, and at the same time, a story of knights capable of taking an honourable part in the international world of chivalry. Bruce's warriors gain their freedom because they are honourable and noble; they are paladins who could be adorning the pages of Froissart's *Chronicles* or an Arthurian romance. The taste of our own times may be more attuned to the wild, romantic savages portrayed in

Braveheart, but Barbour's intention was almost the opposite of Mel Gibson's: he needed to demonstrate that Scotland's leaders were modern and sophisticated. *The Brus* is highly competent within its genre, and it is easy to see why it was a success in its own time. Few readers would enjoy it now, even if the language were modernised, except, perhaps, for the odd moment where profound sentiment ruffles its elegantly enamelled surface. Here is a version in modern English preserving the rhyme, cadence and word order as far as possible. If it seems a little sing-song, it is worth remembering that such poems were written to be read aloud:

> *Ah, Freedom is a noble thing!*
> *Freedom gives man his own liking [choice].*
> *Freedom all solace to man gives;*

> *He lives at ease who freely lives.*
> *A noble heart can have no ease*
> *Nothing there is that can it please*
> *If freedom lacks; for free liking*
> *Is valued over all other things.*
> *He that always has been free*
> *Cannot well know the misery*
> *The anger, and the wretched fate*
> *That links itself with slave's estate.*
> *But if he has been bought and sold*
> *A man loves freedom more than gold.*

Barbour and his poem are commemorated in St Machar's by a set of four wooden panels, created by the wood carver Roland Fraser. Fittingly, this was partly paid for by Aberdeen City Council's 'common good fund', founded by none other than Robert the Bruce, whose other local chari-

Victorian glass-negative photograph of the Chanonry in snow.

table projects may have included the Brig o' Balgownie (see box, p.42).

Medieval Old Aberdeen was a village-sized city, built along the High Street, which continued the line of the way along Spitalhill. Houses on individual plots ran back from the line of the High Street, on either side (see map, p.64). A loop at the northern end, by the cathedral, still called the Chanonry, was where the cathedral canons lived.

The Chanonry

Medieval Scottish bishops were compelled to divide their time between their diocesan duties and the affairs of the kingdom more generally. Highly literate, frequently well versed in law,

they doubled as royal counsellors. It was obvious even in the twelfth century that there would need to be at St Machar's a group of clergy who could run the diocese when the bishop was unavoidably elsewhere; Edward, the second bishop of Aberdeen, received authorisation from Pope Hadrian IV to institute a college of canons at the new cathedral in 1157. Little of their history over the next hundred years can be reconstructed, but by the 1230s there was a team of half a dozen churchmen with clearly defined duties: a dean, who stood in for the bishop when necessary; a precentor, who took care of the seemly conduct of services and all musical matters; a treasurer or bursar; a chancellor, who looked after documents and correspondence with popes, kings, and others, as well as keeping an eye on the cathedral grammar school; an

Brig o' Balgownie

The ancient bridge at Balgownie was and remains one of the sights of Aberdeen. Daniel Defoe observed,

It consists of one immense arch of stone, sprung from two rocks, one on each side, which serve as a buttment to the arch, so that it may be said to have no foundation, nor to need any. The workmanship is artful, and so firm, that it may possibly end with the conflagration only.

By the time the author of *Robinson Crusoe* visited Aberdeen, the bridge was already 400 years old. A variety of stories circulated about its foundation: it was built by Robert the Bruce, according to some, or begun by Bishop Henry Cheyne, who certainly added extensively to the fabric of St Machar's, and finished by the Bruce after Cheyne was forced into exile. Hector Boece's scholarly study of the lives and doings of the bishops of Aberdeen, written in the early sixteenth century, does not mention that Cheyne took a hand in the bridge (though he goes into some detail about Bishop Elphinstone's involvement with the bridge over the Dee). Firmer evidence suggests that it was the council of the royal burgh of Aberdeen who repaired and maintained the bridge.

By the mid-fifteenth century, Balgownie's bridge was in need of repair. As was common in the middle ages, there was a chapel at the bridge end, which performed very much in the nature of a tollbooth, since offerings at the chapel were used for the upkeep of the bridge. In 1443, the chaplain, Sir William Ettale, organised its repair; either he was incompetent or he was not attempting anything more than stop-gap measures, for it was only ten years later that the bridge needed major mason's work, which was authorised by the dean of guild of Aberdeen and cost £31 15s Scots.

No more work was needed for a hundred years or so, but in 1560, money generated by selling silver plate from St Nicholas's was used to pay for the repairs. In post-Reformation Scotland there were no longer bridge chapels, and maintenance and repairs became an ongoing financial headache. Twice, in 1587 and 1596, the burgesses of Aberdeen tried to persuade the Scottish parliament to contribute to the bridge's maintenance costs, on the not-unreasonable grounds that it was a public utility, and necessary for the economic welfare of the entire region.

Parliament ignored them, and by 1604 the bridge was in danger of collapse. Its guardian angel was a member of a local noble family, Sir Alexander Hay of Whytburgh. Perceiving that the problem was bound to recur every few decades, he settled money (£27 8s 8d) in a fund for the upkeep of the bridge in 1605, and a stone plaque recalling his generosity still decorates one of the south-west buttresses. However, in the short term, the bridge needed far more than Hay could give and the cash was scraped together by both fair means and foul: tax funds that had been gathered, in a wave of religious enthusiasm, to send to the Protestants of Geneva were quietly diverted to Balgownie; the presbyteries of Deer and Buchan rattled collection tins to good effect; and the principal of King's raised £96. The bridge was completely rebuilt between 1607 and 1611 by the architect-masons William Massie and Andrew Jameson. Interestingly, Jameson was the father of George Jamesone (1590–1644), who became one of seventeenth-century Britain's most celebrated painters, frequently described as the 'Scottish Van Dyck'. It is fair to suggest that it was the Balgownie bridge job that paid for Jamesone's education. The work was done in three stages, lasting in all more than four years, with known costs in excess of £829: a vast sum in an age when many people lived on less than £5 a year. Though Defoe was clearly under the impression the bridge had stood so firmly since it was built that it would stand till Doomsday, almost everything he saw was the result of this almost complete renewal just a hundred years previously.

Despite the desperate measures which were entered into to pay for the repairs, the burgesses refrained from pillaging Hay's fund, and left it to accrue income. It was first used in 1616 to buy cobbles for the roadway, and in 1704 stood at £713. A hundred years or so later, it was worth more than £20,000.

One of the more significant visitors to Balgownie in the last years of the eighteenth century was George Gordon, Lord Byron. He was brought up in Aberdeen until he was ten, and Balgownie was a favourite walk, as he recalled in a note on his long satirical poem, *Don Juan*:

The brig of Don, near the 'auld toun' of Aberdeen, with its one arch, and its black deep salmon-stream below, is in my memory as yesterday. I still remember, though perhaps I may misquote, the awful proverb which made me pause to cross it, and yet lean over it with childish delight, being an only son, at least by the mother's side. The saying as recollected by me was this, but I have never heard or seen it since I was nine years of age:

Brig of Balgounie, black's *your wa',*
Wi a wife's ae son, and a mear's ae foal,
Doun ye shall fa'!

The prophecy, often ascribed to Thomas the Rhymer, suggests that an only son and a horse which was, similarly, the only foal born to its mother, would be somehow implicated in the ruin of the bridge, a shivery thought for an imaginative child. Byron's love for Balgownie is vivid in the poem itself: twenty-five years after he left Aberdeen, his recollection moved rapidly from the clichés which spelled 'Scottishness' in his own time to what are clearly specific personal memories.

But I am half a Scot by birth, and bred
A whole one, and my heart flies to my head, –
As 'Auld Lang Syne' brings Scotland,
*   one and all,*
Scotch plaids, Scotch snoods, the blue hills,
*   and clear streams,*
The Dee, the Don, Balgounie's Brig's black wall,
All my boy feelings, all my gentler dreams
Of what I *then dreamt, clothed in their own pall,*
Like Banquo's offspring; – floating past me
*   seems*
My childhood in this childishness of mine:
I care not –'tis a glimpse of 'Auld Lang Syne'.

archdeacon who dealt as best he could with the multifarious problems and difficulties of the parish priests, and so spent a great deal of his time out and about in Aberdeenshire; and a legal officer who heard and settled the various kinds of dispute which came to a church court.

As the diocese became richer, more canons were needed. Much of what was gifted to the church, whether by kings or by wealthy laymen, took the form of taxes and other rights, or fishings and lands, which had to be leased out to make a profit. More and more people were needed to cope with the inevitable mountain of paperwork, and by 1445 there were twenty-eight canons, together with procurators, lawyers, surveyors and clerks.

Clearly, the men of the Chanonry could not be supported by the tiny community of Old Aberdeen – which was economically dependent on the cathedral, not vice versa. The system which eventually developed was that each parish within the diocese of Aberdeen provided the stipend, or payment, for one canon. A semicircle of dwelling houses, called manses, was built, fanning out from the cathedral. Each one had some land behind it, and was named after the parish that paid for it. Thus there were the manses of Old Rayne (where John Barbour lived), St Katherine's, Methlick, and so forth. Some of these are known to have been designated for the use of one particular canon. A certain amount of basic furniture came with each house, and each incomer was strictly enjoined to hand it on to his successor, and not to appropriate it as personal property. The earliest evidence for this system dates to the late fourteenth century, by which time (according to the Register of the Bishops of Aberdeen) stone manses were beginning to go up, replacing the relatively ephemeral timber-post-and-wattle structures characteristic of earlier periods. There may have been another burst of building in the fifteenth century, alongside the improvements to the cathedral itself, which also presumably increased the number of canons. But sadly there is no record, either archaeological or archival, which has any light to shed on the lives of the twelfth- and thirteenth-century staff of the cathedral.

By the time of Bishop Elphinstone, the Chanonry was an enclosed community. It had to be; the cathedral had its treasures and medieval Scotland was neither a secure nor a settled society. Even in cities, the houses of the wealthy were small fortresses (see box, p.46), and the towers of St Machar's Cathedral itself have been compared to castellated tower houses of the day. Thomas Orem noted in 1725 that 'this chanry had high strong walls and dikes for defence in troublesome times'. The neighbourhood had four defensive gates: Cluny's Port to the west (a house of which name still stands, fronting onto St Machar Drive, on the spot where the gate once was; see p.24); Bishop's Port to the east, built by Bishop William Stewart and, like Cluny's, surviving into the eighteenth century; a gate across the road leading from Seaton village to the bishop's palace; and a northward gate to Tillydrone Hill. Cluny's Port was decorated with two inscriptions. One, from before the Reformation, said, 'Do not go forth on this road without saying a Hail Mary; you will find forgiveness thus saluting Mary' (*Hac ne vade via, nisi dixeris Ave Maria. Invenies veniam sic salutando Mariam*). Both lines are also found elsewhere: the first was also used as a wall inscription in Paisley, and the second is from a prayer to Mary in the Sarum liturgy that was

Opposite. Granite gradeur in The Chanonry.

Benholm's Lodging, or the Wallace Tower

The building that stands today on Tillydrone Motte in Seaton Park is a cuckoo in the nest of Old Aberdeen. It originally stood in Netherkirkgate in New Aberdeen, where Marks & Spencer now is, and was built by Sir Robert Keith of Benholm, a younger brother of the earl marischal who founded Marischal College. Keith bought the original site in 1588, and built on it some time before his death in 1616 since the property was described in that year as a new house.

Unusually for a town mansion, it is a Z-plan tower house, a version of the castellated structures which Aberdeenshire gentry were putting up all over the county from about 1560. The provision of defensive features such as gun loops under ground-floor windows would have been practical as well as decorative. Another indication of the building's defensive quality is the principal tower, which is more than eight metres tall and is characteristic of the Scots castellated domestic architectural style.

Though subsequently swallowed up by the city of New Aberdeen, Benholm's Tower was built in what was virtually open country, just outside the medieval burgh boundary, some twenty yards west of one of the town gates, Netherkirkgate Port. This may account for its defensive character, since Sir Robert was pursuing an energetic feud with his brother and uncle.

The building's tall sides are decorated with an armorial panel of a kind often found on comparable buildings: as is usual, the largest shield represents the arms of the builder, with crest and the Keith family's supporting stags, all under the motto *Veritas Vincit*, 'Truth Conquers'. The upper shield is indecipherable, but may have shown the cross of St John below the simple motto *Pro Fide*, because the knights of St John, although disbanded at the Reformation, retained the superiority of several properties in Aberdeen.

By far the most unusual feature of the house is a substantial niche containing a stone statue of a man holding a sword, which appears to be part of the original structure. The authors of *Old Landmarks of Aberdeen* quote an Aberdeenshire antiquary's assertion that the figure was taken from a tomb in St Nicholas's kirkyard and set up in the recess by an eighteenth-century owner, John Niven, but this begs the question of what the niche might otherwise have been for. The figure's dress and armour are compatible with the first decade of the seventeenth century, so it is at least possibly a sculpted portrait of the founder of the building, Sir Robert Keith of Benholm. Figures in the round are part of the decoration of a number of Aberdeenshire castles. Tolquhon, in particular, has gate statues of its builder, William Forbes, and his wife; dating from the 1590s, these would have been an obvious model.

In the eighteenth century the building's original name was forgotten and it acquired the name of the Wallace Tower. This was a corruption of well house (local pronunciation would be 'wall hoose') Tower, and derived from

its position near a well at the head of Carnegie's Brae. The stone warrior was accordingly assumed to be William Wallace.

After the death of its builder, the house had a chequered history. It passed into the hands of his brother, the earl marischal, who gave it over for the use of Dr Patrick Dun, appointed principal of Marischal College in 1621, perhaps because of its convenient location less than 200 yards from the college gate. Following Dun's death in about 1631, the house was acquired by William Hay of Balbithan and thereafter it belonged successively to three owners, the last being James Abernethie, merchant. After Abernethie's death in 1768, the plot of land, then called Wallace Nook, was owned by the aforementioned John Niven, a snuff and tobacco merchant. Niven extended the front of the building and added a south wing. In 1789, it passed to James Coutts, and from him to a series of other private owners until 1895, when James Pirie, spirit dealer, acquired the property and converted the basement and ground floor into the Wallace Tower Pub.

The ancient building languished, a neglected slum pub, for half a century, in a run-down area of the city in which the older houses had become tenements. After 1918, the Corporation of the City of Aberdeen became its owners and guardians. Following the Town and Country Planning (Scotland) Act of 1947, the building was listed Category B, indicating its historic and architectural merit. This created a considerable problem when the decision was taken in the mid-1960s to raze the area and build a shopping precinct. Due to its listed status, it was decided that Benholm's Lodging should not be demolished. After intense controversy, it was taken down stone by stone and re-erected out of harm's way in Seaton Park, Old Aberdeen, where it remains the only defensible Z-plan town house in Scotland, as well as the best example of a tower house in either burgh.

promoted by Bishop Elphinstone. A second inscription reflected its rebuilding by Alexander Gordon of Cluny, who gave it his name, in 1623.

One of the problems with the Chanonry's upkeep was persuading the outlying parishes to support it. From a parish point of view, the fact that funds were being diverted from immediate local needs to support an individual in relative luxury at such a distance is unlikely to have been popular. We may guess that it became a grievance from the results. Even in the fifteenth century, there were complaints that the manses were run down and the boundary walls needed to be repaired. The resident canons were instructed to fix the walls or face a penalty.

Bishop William Elphinstone (1431–1514)

Old Aberdeen is as much the creation of a single man as Constantinople. The man in question was William Elphinstone.

In late-medieval Scotland, a university-trained lawyer had to take holy orders in order to pursue his career, and thus could not legally marry. The father of William Elphinstone was such a man, and the future bishop was thus illegitimate, though clearly the product of a relationship his father was not ashamed to acknowledge. Such relationships, which did nothing for the reputation of late-medieval Catholicism, were an almost inevitable result of requiring men who looked towards a career in law, government, or both to do so via the church. According to the eighteenth-century writer George Mackenzie, who seems to have drawn on a lost Elphinstone family tree, Elphinstone's mother was a gentlewoman,

Margaret Douglas, daughter of Sir William Douglas of Drumlanrig.

In 1451, Elphinstone Senior was incorporated as one of the foundation professors of the new University of Glasgow, and elected dean of the faculty of arts there. His son, who lived with him after his earliest years, similarly decided to become a priest, took a degree in canon law at Paris, and then moved on to study civil law at Orléans. At the age of forty he became official (chief legal officer) of the diocese of Glasgow, and like his father before him, the dean of arts a few years later.

By that time the younger Elphinstone's talents had brought him to the attention of the king, James III. He was selected as part of a deputation James sent to Louis XI in 1479, intended to assure the French king that Scottish

Above. The Breviary of Aberdeen, Scotland's first printed book, still resides in Old Aberdeen.

Opposite. Benholm's Lodging in its present location on Tillydrone Motte.

peace negotiations with Edward IV of England in no way undermined Scotland's cordial relationship with France. Louis, unfortunately, was extremely wary of the notion of a rapprochement between the English and the Scots, and managed to wreck the treaty. Elphinstone, who became the chief negotiator, spent much of the 1480s trying to repair it, in discussion with both Richard III and Richard's rival and successor, Henry VII. In gratitude, James III asked the Pope to appoint Elphinstone to the bishopric of Ross in 1481, but he was not consecrated because he could not afford the expense. Transferred to the see of Aberdeen in 1482, he was unable to take up the position for another six years, for the same reason.

By the time of his consecration, Elphinstone was chancellor of Scotland, one of the most senior statesmen and diplomats in the kingdom. But when the king he had served so loyally was overthrown and murdered at Sauchieburn on 11 June 1488, there was no place for him among the men who had thus conspired to put the fifteen-year-old James IV on the throne. He was relieved of his chancellorship, and retired to Aberdeen to concentrate on his pastoral duties. He brought to the task a wealth of political experience, a clear grasp of objectives, and a lawyer's clear, organised mind. He could see perfectly well that the Catholic church of the late fifteenth century badly needed reform. Very well; he had been entrusted with the guidance and

Oil-on-panel portrait of Bishop William Elphinstone, 1505. The depiction of the Aberdeenshire coast, through the open window, left, echoes the words of the university's fifteenth-century mission: to educate the 'rude men . . . cut off from the rest of the kingdom by arms of the sea and very lofty mountains'.

leadership of a part of it, so he would roll up his sleeves and reform it.

Elphinstone's reforms began in 1488, and continued to his death in 1514. Some were local, and some extended to the entire Scottish church. On a local level, he completely reorganised the division of his chapter's funds and laid down the canons' corporate responsibilities and duties. He leaded the roof of his cathedral, completed its central tower, added its steeple, and extended its choir eastwards. He built a bishop's palace, as well as the parish church known since as the Snow Kirk, and began a permanent stone bridge over the River Dee, still extant and in daily use, funding most of it himself.

An action of more national significance was the creation of the Aberdeen Breviary, which introduced the feasts and historical lessons of a selection of Scottish saints to every diocese of the Scottish church. The royal mandate for the foundation of the first printing press in Scotland identified its purpose as the production of 'lawis, actis of parliament, croniclis, mes bukis and portuus [mass books and breviaries], efter the use of our realme'. 'Ane reverend fader in God and our traist [trusty] counsalour, Williame, bischop of Abirdine', is specifically named as the compiler and editor of religious material, and Elphinstone's Breviary (1509) was the first full-sized book which the printers, Chepman and Myllar, actually printed.

Elphinstone himself was an intensely sophisticated man, very aware of new currents of thought (hence his immediate grasp of the possibilities of the new technology of printing), and, like Erasmus, he saw education as the key to

Only the 'gate that leads nowhere' marks the former site of the Bishop's Palace.

reform. The most dramatic result of his overhaul of his diocese was his foundation of the University of Aberdeen. He was absolutely convinced of the need of a university for the North, and went personally to Rome to convince Pope Alexander VI that the remoteness of northern Scotland from any centre of higher learning was creating a serious shortage of lay administrators, doctors of medicine, civil lawyers, and schoolmasters. The Pope confirmed his supplication in a bull of foundation dated 10 February 1495. Teaching began in October 1497, and by 17 September 1505, when King's College received its charter, Elphinstone had collected sufficient funds to support an academic community of thirty-six masters and students (increased to forty-two by 1514), within five faculties: theology, canon and civil law, medicine, and the liberal arts. The first principal, Hector Boece, was a friend of Erasmus.

Though James IV was wary of the men who had supported his father, he found Elphinstone indispensable. He drew Elphinstone back into public life only months after his initial retirement, in October 1488, and for all the energy and activity which the bishop lavished on his see of Aberdeen, he was forced to combine his duties there with sitting as a lawyer, and touring the country with James as a circuit judge. This gave him personal experience of problems in Scots legal procedure and helped him to frame improvements. He also became keeper of the privy seal in 1492, enabling him, with the introduction of the country's first land register, to control one notorious area of corruption in Scottish public life: crown patronage.

For all his immense achievement, Elphin-

Opposite. King's Chapel viewed from the north.

King's College Chapel

King's College Chapel with its elaborate crown spire is one of the most recognisable buildings in Old Aberdeen, indeed, in the country. It was recently voted one of Scotland's favourite buildings in a national poll. Like so much else at King's, it speaks of an ambition and vision which overleaped the modest needs of a university with thirty-six students, to envisage some future point where a great community would come together to sing the praises of God in a magnificent six-bay chapel capable of holding 300. It is the only surviving part of Bishop Elphinstone's original buildings.

The chapel was built on the available open space nearest to the cathedral. The Powis Burn was immediately adjacent (long culverted, it flows underneath Orchard Street) and this was often regarded as a problem. According to Parson Gordon, writing in 1661, 'the foundation of the whole structure resting on slimy and wet ground it was laid on oak beams at great expense and labour.' This seems to be a romantic legend. Excavations by the Aberdeen City Council archaeological unit, undertaken when the chapel's new organ was installed in 2003, revealed a pebble and gravel subsoil, completely stable and suitable for building, and no trace whatsoever of the alleged oak baulks.

Another extremely interesting discovery made at this time was a burial, dated to between AD 1030 and 1220 – centuries before the chapel was begun – suggesting that there may possibly have been an earlier Christian building on the site that has left no trace in written records. The chapel was under construction by 1497–98 when Bishop Elphinstone is known to have bought gunpowder, carts and wheelbarrows in the Netherlands with the help of the Scots agent there, Andrew Halyburton. An inscription on the west front dates the beginning of actual work to 2 April 1500, and the chapel was dedicated in 1509.

One of the major initial decisions taken was to construct most of the building from Moray sandstone, which would have been shipped from Covesea, by Lossiemouth, a sea-trip of more than a hundred miles. This made it a very expensive choice. Granite was and remains the usual local option. Very much easier to carve, sandstone represents the triumph of magnificence over purely practical considerations.

Apart from the crowned spire, the exterior is decorated with an inscription and a variety of armorials, some of which are original (indeed, it is the first building to use the thistle as the king's emblem), carved with a fineness of detail which granite would not have permitted. Elphinstone may have envisaged that more decorative panels would be added over time, and chose his stone accordingly. The lower courses of the walls are of a hard red sandstone of unknown origin, possibly on account of the dampness of the site. Elphinstone got the best workmen he could find: the leadwork of the roof was entrusted to John Burwel, sergeant plumber to the English king, Henry VII.

From the beginning, the plain rectangle of the interior was divided by a rood screen that, as the name suggests, was originally adorned with a great crucifix. It now supports the organ. Within the choir, the choir stalls and canopies, along with the screen itself, are original, the finest surviving sixteenth-century woodwork in Scotland, elaborately carved and decorated, with flamboyant pierced tracery. Space is provided for fifty-two worshippers.

The tower, a massively sturdy construction, was made to house the great bells, and although it is in no sense an afterthought, it stands beside, rather than over, the west end (the tower of St Salvator's College Chapel in St Andrews, the example Elphinstone was probably following, is similarly attached). Its crown, carried by four mighty buttress-like flyers, is a moment of pure architectural virtuosity. A similar crown steeple adorns St Giles' in Edinburgh, and there was once one on St Michael's, Linlithgow. They seem to have been the delight of Scottish church architects around 1500, though they were high-risk structures: Old Aberdeen's original one was blown down in a great gale in 1633. A few days after its fall, one Alexander Wright appeared before the Oldmachar kirk session, accused of calling Bailie Alexander Murray a warlock for raising the wind that destroyed it. The people of the Old Town contributed to putting it up again, suggesting that it was important to local pride.

One feature of the original design which has now disappeared is a two-storey range which lay along the south side, most of the windows on the south side being small and very high as a result. This range housed the sacristy, the treasury or 'jewel house', and the library. Its structure was less sound than that of the chapel itself, since it had to be rebuilt in the mid-1720s and was demolished fifty years later.

The chapel ceased to be used for worship at the Reformation, since the staff and students were meant to go to the kirk – St Machar's. Students were marshalled and marched down the High Street every Sunday, though it was not unknown for some to break ranks, dodge down one of the convenient narrow wynds, and spend the service-time drinking. The Episcopalian tendencies of the college meant that the ban on preaching was not always effective: in 1712, under Principal George Middleton, it was used as an Episcopal church, and in 1761, Principal John Chalmers allowed John Wesley to preach there. It was also used for some degree ceremonies, but all in all, the college was not getting much use out of it. The library was moved into the nave, and would remain there until 1871.

In 1891, the chapel was restored as a place of worship, but the first university chaplain was not appointed until 1945. Thus it is only at the beginning and end of its long history that the building has actually been used for worship. Though relatively few of today's students attend services there, the enormous numbers who return to King's for their weddings suggests that it is a building many of them nonetheless care about. It is also at the heart of the university's musical life, with concerts and recitals held regularly.

Sacrist Stan Jack at the chapel's west door.

stone's life ended in tragedy. He had hoped in 1502 that he had finally achieved a lasting peace with England, but it was destroyed by Henry VIII's aggressively anti-French policies. James IV, against Elphinstone's vehement opposition, accepted Louis XI's argument that he was honour-bound by the terms of the 'Auld Alliance' to challenge the English king in the field. James was killed, along with most of his nobility, at the battle of Flodden in 1513.

Elphinstone's reputation as an elder statesman of incorruptible honour was confirmed when he was subsequently appointed guardian of the infant James V, and nominated to the metropolitan see of St Andrews (which would have been easier to combine with participation in a caretaker government). But he died, worn out, just over a year after James IV, on 25 October 1514, working to the last on the restoration of the country's political and legal stability after total military defeat. He was buried at the foot of the sanctuary in his chapel (see box, p.52) at King's College, Old Aberdeen.

Elphinstone's successor as bishop, Gavin Dunbar, was not known for his parsimony, but he truly spared no expense when it came to Elphinstone's tomb. In contrast to the plain stone slab which stands in front of the altar in the chapel today, this was a grandiose monument in marble and bronze in the latest Renaissance taste, with an effigy of the bishop; it was destroyed during the civil wars. Had things gone differently in Scotland, Elphinstone might well have come to be honoured as a saint. Hector Boece, in his *Life*, provided a hearty nudge in that direction with his account of the great bishop, which emphasises his 'innocent youth, illustrious manhood . . . faultless old age', and lifelong devotion to the Virgin. Boece also

recounted a series of miracles that took place at Elphinstone's burial: his crosier unaccountably broke and part of it fell into the grave, all the weathervanes fell off the churches, and a mysterious voice was heard. If Elphinstone had been established as a saint, then King's Chapel, with its crown and its great bells (see box opposite), would have become his shrine, a place of pilgrimage and devotion. We may never know for certain, but the anticipation of sainthood would go a long way toward explaining the money and labour that were expended on the physical splendours of the place.

For five centuries, despite the Reformation, the university has stubbornly continued to mark the death-day of a man who was not only a local benefactor, but one of the great statesmen and patriots of the nation's history.

The People of Old Aberdeen

Not every resident of Old Aberdeen was connected with either the city or the college. In contrast to the well-recorded evolution of St Machar's and the Chanonry, the development of the city of Old Aberdeen between the twelfth and the fifteenth centuries is almost entirely obscure. We do know, however, that it had a modest commercial life of its own in the middle ages, independent of New Aberdeen. Once it had been incorporated as a burgh (at Elphinstone's instigation), Old Aberdeen's burgesses had the right to hold a weekly market and two annual fairs. Since there was no room for a marketplace, traders' booths were crammed into the High Street. Even now, the street is wider in front of the Town House, and the remains of a market cross (see box, p.56) still stands there.

Bells

It is fitting for the inhabitants of a cathedral city to be summoned by bells. The inhabitants of Old Aberdeen were particularly well off in this respect. In a world without domestic clocks and watches, medieval church bells were used to call the faithful to mass, alert the population to danger, and ring the dead to their long journey home. Like much else in Old Aberdeen, Bishop Elphinstone's bells were surprisingly magnificent. When he built a centre tower onto St Machar's, he placed in it fourteen 'tuneable and costly' bells, three of which weighed more than half a ton apiece. Such big bells were enormously expensive, and installing objects of such great size and weight high above the ground was no mean challenge, but it was done, and their sweet, full tones could be heard over great distances.

Bells, like ships, were so expensive and took such an enormous amount of highly skilled and specialised labour to create that they normally acquired names and on their installation were ceremonially blessed with oil, salt and wine. Their strong associations with Catholic worship sealed their fate at the Reformation: in 1568 the earl of Moray ordered their removal, along with the lead from the cathedral roof. Interestingly, the Aberdonians flatly refused to participate and the job had to be done by a burgess of Edinburgh, William Birnie, who loaded lead and bells alike into a ship, intending to sell them in Holland to raise money for the regent's troops. The ship was lost with all hands, Birnie included, on its way to the Low Countries, probably due to overloading rather than divine wrath, though there would have been those who wondered.

King's was even more magnificently equipped. In 1521, Hector Boece boasted of the college's 'thirteen bells pleasing the ear with sweet and holy melody', then brand new. Since King's was primarily an educational rather than a religious institution, its bells escaped the reformers' zeal. We know the names of the five great bells: Trinity, Maria, Michael, Gabriel, and Raphael. The three largest were made in the Low Countries, and signed by a member of a dynasty of bellfounders in Mechelen who exported all over Europe: 'I am called Gabriel: sing to the Lord a new song. Sing with all your skill to Him with a joyful noise. By me, George Waegheren, in the year of our Lord 1519.' Trinity and Maria were the two largest. Trinity weighed two and a half tons, and stood over five feet high, which made it the biggest bell in Scotland in its day. These great bells have gone, but there is a surviving Waegheren bell in Perth, made by George's brother Peter. Called John the Baptist, it dates to 1506.

The college day was marked by the tolling of bells. At 5 a.m. the sacrist rang for fifteen minutes to wake staff and students alike, while another bell, rung at 5 a.m. in winter and 4 a.m. in the summer, was used to signal the opening of the college gate, and was heard again at 9 in the evening, when the college was closed and locked. The morning service of matins was announced at 6 a.m., as was the beginning of lectures, by a less dignified bell that acquired the name Clatter Vengeance, since it could be rung a different way to make a very different sound and its second voice was used to summon the students to 'discipline', the minute enquiry into belief and personal morality which was a

principal tool of the Kirk's control over individual lives. Students quite often have a fair amount on their consciences, hence the name. Katherine Trail, who spent her childhood in a house on the High Street, recalled that even in the 1870s, Clatter Vengeance was 'generally the first sound we heard in the morning'.

Part of the reason why the enormous bells were used only on special occasions was that they were easily damaged. Because of the colossal forces involved, they could be cracked by a careless ringer and their tone ruined. By 1700, nobody dared to ring the great bells at all, and a bell-founder of French origin, M. Albert Gelly, offered to recast them. One of Gelly's small bells, dated 1702, still survives, and was used as the curfew bell as late as the nineteenth century. The only one of Bishop Elphinstone's bells still surviving is, again, one of the small ones: less than two feet high, it was made by a London founder called William Culverden before 1522.

The enormous size and magnificence of the college bells, far beyond any reasonable need of the college per se, is a mystery in itself. Elphinstone's cathedral bells were splendour sufficient, or so one might have thought. Pace Hector Boece, who attributed them to Elphinstone, the college bells can only have been installed by his successor as bishop, Gavin Dunbar, who laboured mightily to complete Elphinstone's great projects: the bridge over the Dee, the refurbishment of St Machar's, and King's College. By 1519, the date of Waegheren's bells, Elphinstone had been dead for five years.

The Mercat Cross

When Old Aberdeen became a burgh of barony in the late fifteenth century, it acquired the right to its own market, and consequently required a mercat cross to indicate the designated area – the widest point of the High Street. As well as indicating a market, a mercat cross marked a burgh's place of public assembly in a more general sense: in a world in which news was brought to the people orally, the mercat cross was the location where proclamations were made, and also where public punishments were meted out.

The actual cross of Old Aberdeen probably dates from around 1540. It was originally highly decorative: topped by a crucifix, it also bore images of the Virgin on the north and south sides, together with representations of the coats of arms of the kings of Scotland and of bishops Dunbar, Stewart and Gordon. The images of the Virgin were defaced at the time of the Reformation, in 1560, though the crucifix otherwise remained more or less intact until it was destroyed during the civil wars. In the 1780s the council of Old Aberdeen sold the cross, but when the remains of the heraldic knop turned up in a smithy in Old Aberdeen in 1841, it was carefully kept, and in 1951, the university put it back on top of a shaft in front of St Mary's Church in the High Street. Its last move was in 1993, when it was transferred back to its current – and original – location.

Left. The Mercat Cross today.

Opposite. Forty miles to the north, in Banff, a rare survival indicates how Old Aberdeen's Cross might have once looked.

Opposite. Late afternoon
81 The High Street.

The cathedral and its personnel lived in a world of their own, enclosed behind the walls of the Chanonry: a world of men and boys. From the fifteenth century onwards, so did the professors and students of King's: a similar bachelor society, confined, as far as was practicable, behind the walls of the college bounds, using Latin as the language of their daily lives as well as of their studies.

Located between these two worlds of men and Latin was what was called the 'Middle Toun', the world of the burgh of Old Aberdeen in all its variety: craftsmen, layabouts, wifies, babies, rude children, trollops, old people and prentices, buying, selling, and going about their business in the vigorous North-east Scots vernacular. The layout established in the Middle Ages is still preserved in today's High Street: two rows of dwellings faced each other, crowded together, and roofed with thatch. Each stood at the head of a 'rig', a long strip of land used for vegetable-growing, stabling, poultry-keeping, clothes-drying, and workshop space. The earliest houses would have been timber-framed and thatch-roofed, their walls built up with wattle and daub. Houses of this type dating from the late twelfth to the early fourteenth century have been excavated in Aberdeen. It was thus the standard building type at the time when the town was coming together, though direct evidence for it in Old Aberdeen is, unavoidably, entombed beneath the extant houses of the High Street.

The Middle Toun, like the Chanonry and the college, was enclosed for reasons of security; even this far east, it was not unknown for Highland caterans to raid and drive off cattle. It was not actually walled, but back dykes ran along the far ends of the gardens, and formed a continuous defensive barrier, each householder being responsible for the maintenance of his own section. One of the early town council statutes, dating from 1603, exhorts the inhabitants to 'bige [build] upe the bakdykis for outhalding of strangeres of [from] this towne'. The burgh also owned common fields, beyond the back dykes, where the householders grazed their cattle. They were vulnerable to theft, so a professional herdsman acted as 'cow-sitter'. The animals' owners paid him eightpence per week per cow.

A soft bluish haze of peat smoke hung over the city. Peat rather than coal was the usual fuel, since there was a peat moss outside the town. The nostalgic smell overlay less pleasant odours of excrement and foul middens (which the residents preferred to site in the common street rather than in their own backyards), and pigs, chickens and horses all contributed their characteristic odours. The town's butchers were in the habit of slaughtering cattle, pigs and sheep in the middle of the High Street, a practice which was not forbidden until 1754, so often enough the vennels will have run red with blood and offal. The town council did their best to ensure that the water supply remained drinkable by forbidding any kind of washing upstream of the town.

An obvious driver of the little city's prosperity was St Machar's, a busy building site from the twelfth century onwards. King James's charter incorporating Old Aberdeen as a free burgh of barony in 1489, allowed its inhabitants 'full power and liberty to buy and sell within the said burgh wines, wax, cloth woollen and linen, broad and narrow, and other merchandise; and to have and to hold bakers, brewers, sellers of flesh and fish, and other craftsmen in any way belonging to the freedom of the burgh of

barony'. Purveyors of food were obviously necessary, and it was a great convenience for the community around St Machar's to have them within reach, but the 'other craftsmen' must have loomed large: masons, above all, and men who worked with wood, stone or metal in myriad complex and specialist ways. Horses had to be shod, so there had to have been a smithy. One slightly surprising specialist craftsman who established himself in Old Aberdeen in the second half of the sixteenth century was an armourer, Matthew Guild, who became wealthy and influential, though he can have had few customers within the burgh. North-west of the town was a watermill, taking advantage of a fast-running burn: this was referred to as Gordonsmill in 1608 and is on Parson Gordon's 1661 map, but could well have been much older, since there were watermills in Scotland from at least the twelfth century.

Old Aberdeen and the Reformation

Abundant evidence suggests that the late-medieval Catholic church in Scotland was, for the most part, profoundly inadequate. The fact that many churchmen were in effect lawyers, or politicians, or otherwise doing good service to the state in the absence of a secular professional class, is something which we can see in retrospect. But many of them made a mockery of their vows and, considered as spiritual leaders, they were on the whole a scandalous bunch.

It was a church ripe for reform – with one obvious exception. The people of Old Aberdeen had more reason than those of any other burgh in Scotland to view the Catholic church with unqualified approval. Their city was a burgh of

barony, for the great William Elphinstone had won them their independence from New Aberdeen. His successor, Dunbar, had endowed a hospital, and built upon Elphinstone's beginnings with respect to their great cathedral and their university. The prosperity of the burgh revolved, in other words, around effective, zealous and entrepreneurial Catholic bishops – who were also the barons. Everything the people had, everything they were proud of, came directly from the Church. In the wider diocese, many may have resented paying tithes and other exactions to support the manses of the Chanonry, but much of the money which flowed into the Church's coffers was spent in Old Aberdeen. The cathedral and, from the end of

the fifteenth century, the college were constantly being developed, bringing work to the burgh's craftsmen and labourers. The welling up of genuine, grassroots-level exasperation which fuelled the Reformation in most of Scotland was probably less felt in Old Aberdeen than anywhere else, and it is quite easy to see why.

The Scottish parliament, when it met in July and August 1560, abolished papal authority throughout the realm, forbade the celebration of the mass, and recognised the sole competence of a Reformed ministry in ecclesiastical affairs. In St Andrews the year before, John Knox had led an enthusiastic mob to destroy the 'rags of popery' in St Rule's Cathedral, which remains to this day a ruined, albeit magnificent, shell. There

Opposite. Looking southward into the burgh from St Machar Drive.

Above. The skills that built the burgh are still in evidence.

61

was no such feeling discernible in Aberdeen: the earl of Huntly, Leslie of Balquhain and their followers arrived in time to prevent reformers (who had entered Aberdeenshire for the purpose) from razing St Machar's Cathedral, as had been done in St Andrews and Elgin. Our Lady of Aberdeen was taken down and kept, probably by Huntly, until she could be sent over to the Spanish Netherlands, but this was not until 1625. One of very few surviving three-dimensional sculptures from medieval Scotland to survive, she is still in Brussels, though a copy can be seen in the Lady Chapel of St Mary's Catholic Cathedral in New Aberdeen. At least one of the cathedral's four altars to Our Lady survived the Reformation as well: according to Thomas Orem (see box, p.64), 'the portrait of our Blissid virgyn Marie and hir deir sone babie Jesus in hir armes, that had stood since the up-putting theirof, in curious wark' was not taken down until the 1640s.

Bishop Gordon, a younger son of the third earl of Huntly, was no Bishop Elphinstone. In fact, he illustrated rather precisely the problems which could result from giving ecclesiastical preferment to well-born younger sons. He was a learned man, a lawyer educated at King's, Paris and Angers. Genuinely concerned about the training and moral laxity of his clerics, he did what he could to combat the spread of heresy. He was the first bishop in Scotland to implement the decrees of the Council of Trent, the Catholic Church's own modernisation programme, and draw up a scheme of reform based on its recommendations. Unfortunately, his exhortations may have rung a little hollow since he had imprudently become the father of five sons and three daughters, all of whom had to be provided for out of diocesan funds.

Despite being in effect married (all of his eight children had the same mother), he was orthodox on all other issues and was generally respected. He personally attended the provincial council convened in 1549 to undertake the reform of the Scottish church, and when the Catholic Mary, Queen of Scots arrived from France in 1561, both he and his highly conservative diocese must have had hopes that the Protestants' pretensions would be swept away. But a mere six years later, it was the queen who was swept away: forced to abdicate, her power passed to her Protestant half-brother, the regent Moray, and the reformers' agenda triumphed.

Clergy who would not subscribe to the new Protestant confession of faith were relieved of their ministry. Their positions were given to those who could square the Reformed faith with their consciences. Bishop Gordon showed a certain elasticity on this point. He refused to step down, and for the ten years that followed, survived all attempts to remove him from office. He died, as he had lived, in his palace, on 6 August 1577, and was buried in his cathedral church of St Machar. His successor, David Cunningham, was a convinced Protestant, who had been the chaplain to Moray's successor as regent, the fourth earl of Morton. Morton was thought by some contemporaries to be insufficiently reformist since he was in favour of retaining bishops rather than going all the way with Calvin and embracing the principles of Presbyterianism, but he was certainly a Protestant.

Even in New Aberdeen, the forces of religious conservatism were strong. The burgesses and the magnates brought themselves to sign the bond of the Congregation in 1560, but the man they chose as first minister of the Reformed Kirk in the New Town was Adam Heriot, a shy and retiring scholar, not a fiery rabble-rouser in the mode of John Knox. Unlike anywhere else in Scotland, Aberdeen drifted gradually and half-heartedly into Protestantism. The Catholic clergy were not forced to leave the burgh; in fact, the Menzies family, who virtually ruled New Aberdeen in the sixteenth century, bought up the treasures of the parish church and kept on the former prior of the town's Carmelite monastery as a private chaplain. Even after 1560 it was not at all difficult to attend mass and receive the sacraments.

St Machar's, grudgingly preserved, became Old Aberdeen's parish church, but the building was so large in relation to its congregation that it was impossible to keep fully weathertight, especially after the lead had been removed by order of the earl of Moray in 1568. The roof was not slated until thirty-nine years later, so it is just as well that the wooden ceiling was of superlative workmanship. It is a testimony to the obstinate conservatism of Old Aberdeen that it was not until 1640 (under the reforming principal, William Guild, who had been intruded in the place of a predecessor who refused to sign the Covenant) that the arms of Christ and other Catholic symbols were chiselled out of the building's fabric. The cathedral had, by that time, been a place of Protestant worship for sixty years.

King's College, meanwhile, was facing a similar problem. It had been founded as a community of men in holy orders, and it remained a Catholic university until 1569, when the regent Moray, as a side-issue to disciplining the earl of Huntly, purged the college of its principal, Alexander Anderson, and four other professors who refused to sign the new

Opposite. Bishop Dunbar's sixteenth-century personal arms still grace this ancient and much-modified house in the Chanonry.

Mr Orem's Curiosities

One of the principal sources of information on Old Aberdeen in the seventeenth and eighteenth centuries circulated for years under a false attribution. *A Description of the Chanonry, Cathedral and King's College of Old Aberdeen, in the years 1724 and 1725* passed from hand to hand in the eighteenth century, being added to anonymously as it went, until a copy was acquired by the topographer Richard Gough. Gough published it as the work of the town clerk of Old Aberdeen, William Orem, a mistake repeated in later editions.

In fact, the author of the account was an antiquarian of independent means, Thomas Orem, who died in 1730. The earliest mention of him relates to his marriage in Kemnay parish, Aberdeenshire, in 1693. He lived in Old Aberdeen from 1698 until his death, being made an honorary burgess in 1702.

Apart from the valuable transcripts of ancient documents which Orem's work contains, the *Description* is a wonderful core sample of the mentality of an educated northern Scot of the early eighteenth century. Orem was Episcopalian in religion and profoundly conservative in politics. His was a quiet, eirenic Lutheranism, profoundly hostile to the socially turbulent theocracy of Calvinism with its breaches of decorum, and not without nostalgia for the benefactions and decencies of Catholicism. His chronicle does not even have an entry for the 1715 Jacobite rising, except to note that Old Aberdeen was subsequently fortified

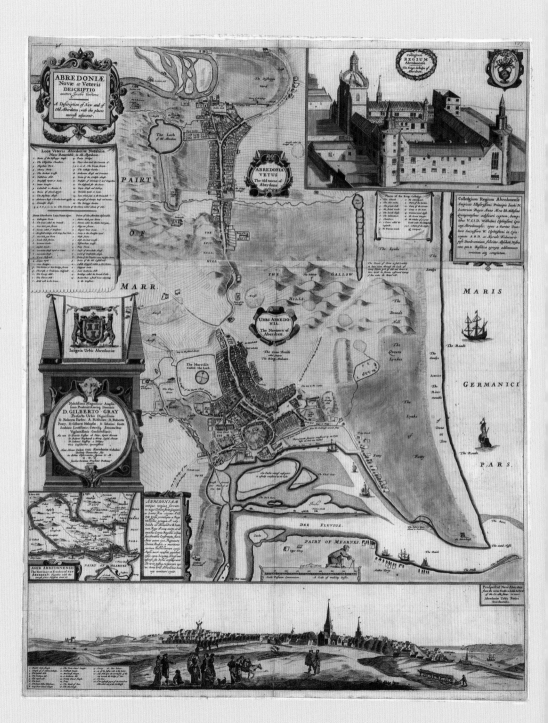

Parson Gordon's map of Old Aberdeen in 1661, showing the position of the loch.

against the Highlanders, though his unremitting nostalgia, his love for times past and his pleasure in the survival of old customs and old usages would suggest that he shared, discreetly and privately, the Stuart loyalism which characterised Aberdeen and Aberdeenshire from the mid-seventeenth century to the mid-eighteenth.

One of the real pleasures of Orem's account (and the anonymous contributions which it attracted) is in the recording of small details of life and memory of the kind which had fascinated the English antiquarian John Aubrey: 'How these curiosities would be quite forgott, did not such idle fellowes as I am put them downe!' So it is fitting that Orem recorded that pictures in King's College Hall consisted in part of a series of bishops of Aberdeen, Catholic merging seamlessly into Reformed:

The hall is ornamented with
some tolerable portraits. Over
the chimney, bishops Elphinston
and Dunbar, copied from
originals in the principal's lodge.
Bishops Forbes, Leslie and
Scougal[.]

Indeed, these can be identified with those paintings framed in series with gold frames carved with oak leaves, now in the collection of the university. It is extra-ordinary, and very Aberdonian, that the series should emphasise continuity, not disjunction. John Lesley, the resistant Catholic, apologist for Mary Queen of Scots, and eventual bishop of Coutances in Normandy, simply holds his place on the wall despite religious and political changes. He had been a professor at King's, after all.

Similarly, Orem recorded the museum of King's College, nascent in the ordered preservation of 'curiosities' in the library (at that time still housed in the lean-to range abutting the college chapel):

In it is an ancient plan of
Aberdeen by James Gordon,
and a silver penny of one of the
Scottish Kings found here;
several missals, ancient and
foreign arms, and sundry
natural curiosities.

It is tempting to associate with these curiosities an otherwise unexplained engraved plate of fossil and mineral specimens, including a chambered nautilus, printed alongside Orem's text.

In many ancient European universities, the graduate or 'laureate' was literally crowned with laurel or flowers. Aberdeen seems to have had its own variant of this practice in the early seventeenth century, when the winner of the competition for the best Latin verses was crowned with flowers, providing an explanation for the roses and carnations which, in some of George Jamesone's portraits, offer such a puzzling contrast to the sober black broadcloth of the sitters.

The ivory crown of ivory flowers
was made by Mrs Lees, whose
husband was a principal man of
advocate Black's factory in
Aberdeen. This crown is large,
and is made up of several sorts
of coloured flowers, which the
students in the magistrand class
bought, and gave her sixty
pounds Scots for it. It hangs

yearly in the common school, in
time of graduations, and at other
times in the bibliotheck.

Orem mentioned with pleasure the use which Sir Alexander Gordon of Cluny made of Old Aberdeen's loch (now the playing fields of St Machar Academy) and the little island in it. As well as his extensive garden at Cluny's Port with its clipped-box parterres in the form of saltires and quincunxes of trees set in grass, Sir Alexander

when he lived in the Chanry . . .
had a summer-house in the
middle of the said loch, and
a pleasure boat upon it, for
passing and re-passing to the
said summer-house.

As every early-modern antiquarian should, Orem also paid heed to ghost stories. The manse of the parson of Clatt, located on the west side of the Chanonry

. . . was called Tam Framper's
house because it was haunted.
The deceast George Cruick-
shank carried away some of
the stones . . . and when the
Englishmen came hither they
carried away the rest.

'Tam Framper' would seem to be a traditional name for a demon.

Confession of Faith. Moray began turning King's into a Protestant university under an intruded principal, Alexander Arbuthnot. It was a careful choice. Arbuthnot was a man of great learning and considerable charm, educated at St Andrews and Bourges, and in a quiet way one of Old Aberdeen's many poets (see box, p.68). James Melville described him as 'a man of singular gifts of lerning, wisdome, godliness, and sweitnes of nature'. His was a position requiring massive reserves of tact and diplomacy, and he seems to have been the right man for the job, which he held until his death in 1585.

Old Aberdeen remained highly conservative, and Episcopalian in preference, into the seven-

teenth century. A significant number of gentry Catholics lived unmolested in the Chanonry, under the protection of the first marquis of Huntly and his wife Henrietta, daughter of the duke of Lennox, who had been raised entirely in France and was inflexibly Catholic. The Protestant bishops continued to be important people in the town; the tendency of the churchmen who came to Old Aberdeen was to be far more tolerant of royal intervention in religion, and of various shades of religious preference, than the doctrinaire Presbyterians who ruled the kirk further to the south. The most important Old Aberdeen cleric, Patrick Forbes of Corse (1564–1635), was described by

From left to right: classrooms, the divinity library, and porter's lodge, King's College. Seen from the north-east.

Old Aberdeen Poets

John Barbour has already been mentioned as the poet of
Scotland's independence. He, or another canon of St
Machar's, also wrote a long versification of the lives of
the saints some time in the fourteenth century. The next
noteworthy poet of Old Aberdeen flourished 200 years
later. He was Alexander Arbuthnot, elected principal of
King's College in 1569, the first Protestant head of the
college. He was an extremely learned man who had studied
both at King's and at the University of Bourges, and a
poet in both Latin and English. Arbuthnot's vernacular
verse includes, somewhat unexpectedly, a long poem
standing up for women, of which this is a fair sample:

> Quhen God maid all of nocht
> He did this weill declare,
> The last thing that he wrocht
> It was a woman fair.
> In workes we see the last to be
> Maist plesand and preclair [notable]
> An help to man God maid her than:
> Quhat will ye I say mair?

This is light verse, suggesting a pleasant and genial
personality. His other long poem, *The Miseries of a Pure
Scholar* (1572), looked at the troubles of academic life,
squabbles in the college community and the need to
scrabble for a job or please a patron. Much of what he
wrote has its resonances even today, but he reflected a
dilemma particularly characteristic of pre-modern
Scotland when he wrote,

> I luif justice, and wald that everie man
> Had that quhilk richtlie does him to perteine;
> Yet all my kyn, allya [alliance], or my clan
> In richt or wrang, I man [must] alwayis mantene.

The poets of the seventeenth century mostly wrote in Latin.
John Johnston, who studied at King's, was one of the
earliest, but another Johnston – Arthur – was probably the
best. Born at Caskieben in Aberdeenshire and educated
at King's, his greatest work was a poem in praise of
his birthplace,

> Where with the thousand glimmering sequins of
>   her waters
> The Urie trembles between her happy fields,
> And where the great mass of Bennachie spreads
>   all around the shadows of evening,
> Where night is weighed in the balance,
>   and equals the day.

Several seventeenth-century King's professors wrote
poetry. Alexander Garden, professor of philosophy,
published two collections, *Theatre of the Scotish Kings*
and *A Garden of Grave and Godly Flowers*, while John
Lundie, humanist, wrote gracefully on the death of the
much-loved bishop of Aberdeen, Patrick Forbes.

Both the sons of the second marquis of Huntly, George
and Charles Gordon, were King's alumni and staunch
royalists. George, the elder, was killed commanding the
right wing of Montrose's army at the battle of Alford in
1645, and Charles (Lord Aboyne) fought on for King
Charles's cause until he was beheaded in 1649. Typically
for Cavalier poets, they wrote love songs, satires against
the king's enemies and poems in praise of his friends.

The Jacobite risings in their turn drew a variety of
poetical responses from Aberdeenshire. George Halket, a
King's alumnus, wrote one of the best known, 'Whirry
Whigs Awa'', and 'A Dialogue between the Devil and
George II', which apparently caused the duke of
Cumberland to offer a reward of £100 for the author dead
or alive. Halket also wrote the classic love lyric 'Logie o'
Buchan', reckoned among the dozen or so best Lowland
Scottish songs. The strongly Jacobite views of John Ker,
professor of Greek at King's, were expressed more
discreetly, in Latin. He also published *Donaides*, a poem
celebrating the distinguished dons and alumni of Aberdeen
University.

A noted Aberdeen character who kept the Jacobite
cause alive until he died, aged over 100 years, was
'Mussel-mou'd Charlie', so called from an odd deformity of
his lower lip. His real name was Charles Lesly, and he
claimed to have been 'out' with the Jacobite armies in both
the Fifteen and the Forty-Five. Until his eventual death in
1782, he wandered the two Aberdeens with 'a large

Mussel-mou'd Charlie.

harden bag, hung over his shoulder', full of printed ballads, which he sang 'in a deep and hollow roar', and sold to the townsfolk. Asked, 'Why cannot you sing other songs than those rebellious ones?' by a Hanoverian provost, Charles is said to have replied, 'Oh aye, but – they winna buy them!'

The most significant poet of eighteenth-century Old Aberdeen was also a ballad singer, though of a very different kind. Anna Gordon (1747–1810) was the daughter of the professor of humanities at King's. Her mother was the daughter of the Aberdeenshire composer Forbes of Disblair, and she grew up in a richly musical environment. She was a singer of traditional ballads, but since her versions are almost uniformly superior to those of other singers, it is clear that her role was a genuinely creative one: she sang old stories to old tunes, but gave them an individuality, beauty and pathos which came from her own taste and judgment. No fewer than twenty-seven of the principal or most complete texts in Francis James Child's definitive collection, *English and Scottish Popular Ballads*, are hers. She treats the traditional ballads from an explicitly female, even feminist, perspective, illustrating the hazards of women's lives, as well as the courage, resolve and intelligence of individual heroines.

While George Macdonald is now chiefly remembered as a novelist, his first book, *Within and Without*, was a novel in verse, and he published poetry throughout his life that was much read in its day.

Twentieth-century Old Aberdeen's most notable poet was Olive Fraser (1909–77). A woman of tremendous natural talent, her considerable early success (she won more than twenty literary prizes) was overshadowed by the development of a thyroid condition which went undiagnosed for four decades. Because her condition was misunderstood, she spent much of her life in and out of mental hospitals, but she battled on as best she could, and continued to write. Her best work is stark, individual and passionate. Twelve years after her death, her collected poems were published under the title *The Wrong Music*.

Melville as 'guid, godlie, and kynd'. He became a bishop with some reluctance, but in the event exercised the office with great diligence, and also set about major reforms of the finances and instruction at King's.

Forbes's death was met with an outpouring of regret from town and gown alike, printed in a large book by Edward Raban (d. 1658), printer in New Aberdeen, who was pleased to acknowledge how much he personally owed to the bishop. In a little coda to the volume, Raban wrote,

> *Good sirs, I am behind the rest*
> *I doe confesse, for want of skill.*
> *But not a whit behind the best*
> *To show th'affection of good will.*

Seventeenth-century Life

After the Reformation, the burgh court book, which begins in 1602, and the kirk session register, which begins in 1621, between them give a picture of the people and their doings. A census of 1636 reveals the tiny size of the burgh (some 900 souls): it is sobering to think that it was the second largest burgh in Aberdeenshire after New Aberdeen down to the end of the eighteenth century, when it was overtaken by Peterhead, and indicates how very small the population was overall. The purpose of the 1636 census was to allow a jury of thirty of the oldest and most respected citizens to identify 'begaris ydleris and vagabounds' among the folk of the burgh, and either to expel them or compel them to amend their lives. In so doing, it reveals much of the life of the Middle Toun.

In contrast to the all-male communities of St Machar's and King's immediately to the north and south, much of the Middle Toun was female. There were 193 households, 134 of which contained a housewife, together with ninety-three female servants (some 10 per cent of the total population). But not all women were housewives or servants: fifty-one Middle Toun women were the heads of their households, and many of this group did not define themselves as housewives, but plied a definite trade, mostly making or vending some particular foodstuff, or working with textiles. There were poor women living in pairs or alone, and seventeen households which consisted of a mother and her children – widows, not 'single mothers', since they were evidently persons of good repute in seventeenth-century terms. It was observed in the eighteenth century that there were an unusual number of widows and older single women in Old Aberdeen. It was easy to get work, stocking-knitting in particular (there were already four 'shankers', or stocking-knitters, in the 1636 census), and because the town was so compact, it was also easy for an old lady to buy food and other necessities. The records for the seventeenth century suggest that the Middle Toun was already attractive to women struggling along without a husband – and within the context of those more troubled times, it is worth adding that it was relatively safe. Town council minutes, recording scoldings and 'flytings' certainly suggest that the town was not lacking in strong-minded and wilful wifies.

In the burgh population as a whole, the largest occupation group was the weavers, identified as central to Old Aberdeen's economic life in James IV's charter of 1489. These 'wobsters' were the most prominent and wealthiest of the burgh's five craft guilds: by

1677, there were so many people selling cloth on market day that there was no room to get down the street for all the booths, and the council decided to create a designated cloth market, extending to Cluny's Port along what is now St Machar Drive. The importance of the weavers is also directly indicated by the various crafts' contributions to the salary of the master of the cathedral song school. The weavers gave ten merks, twice as much as any of the other crafts. David Abell, the deacon of the guild of weavers in 1636, had nine servants in his house, more than any other resident of the city. The other four guilds were the shoemakers – called 'cordiners', in Scots – tailors, butchers or 'fleshers', and hammermen. This last designation covered wrights, coopers and smiths, all of whom, in one way or another, relied on hammering for their living. There were, of course, spinsters, since this was the default occupation of unmarried women. Other townsfolk made or sold bread and brewed ale; one woman appears in the census as a 'pudding-wright', probably a sausage-maker. The 'muckster' dealt as best he could with the town's accumulation of excrement, human and animal. Some occupations hint at the specialist needs of the college; a candlemaker may have had customers at King's, since thrifty housewives made their own tallow dips, and a bookbinder

almost certainly looked principally to the college for his commissions. The midwife, on the other hand, had no business there, or so it was to be hoped.

Beggars were a continual problem. It may be that the tenacity of folk memory brought beggars in unusual numbers to Old Aberdeen, since, before the Reformation, Catholic ideas of charity had probably extended to food doles, if perhaps no more. The town council was very exercised throughout the century about strangers coming in with no visible means of support; a miniature and local version of today's worries about immigrants. Penalties were levied against those townsfolk who took strangers in without making proper enquiry, and 'sturdy' beggars were periodically flushed out – or found work. In 1643, an Old Aberdeen couple committed themselves to taking on a woman called Elspet Gilchrist, who had been begging in the town, as an apprentice: they agreed to feed and clothe her for seven years, and to teach her to make stockings.

Though by and large the burgh was inhabited by artisans and people of a modest way of life, the gentry formed a small but extremely visible part of Old Aberdeen's population. The most important of these were Gordons. The earls of Huntly, who had remained Catholic, had a residence in the Chanonry by the second half of the sixteenth century, and protected a community of Catholic and conservative sympathisers who lived there. These included their close relation Bishop William Gordon, second son of the third earl, who, as we have seen, survived all attempts to dislodge him and died in his palace in 1577. The Chanonry was notoriously a place where mass was regularly celebrated. The fourth earl welcomed English rebels, refugees from the failed rising against Elizabeth in 1569, to his house in Old Aberdeen. The devoutly Catholic Anne Percy, née Somerset, countess of Northumberland, stayed for some time with Lord Seton, head of another Aberdeenshire noble family with a house in Old Aberdeen, and heard mass there every day. The Catholic eighth earl of Errol acquired a Chanonry manse in 1588.

Another prominent man of Old Aberdeen at the beginning of the seventeenth century was Sir Alexander Gordon of Cluny. He was a nephew of the third earl of Huntly, but hailed from a Protestant branch of the family. Like his father Sir Thomas, he was prominent in Old Aberdeen affairs, and served as provost for many years. He bought the manse of Invernochty, and later acquired the adjacent manses and gardens of Turriff and Methlick and combined the three properties to make a substantial enclosed garden in 1623 that extended towards the loch to the west. He also built a gallery and joined it with the chamber above the west gate of the Chanonry, which became known as 'Cluny's Port' after his rebuilding.

The burgh's attractiveness for widows was also noticeable at gentry level. Four gentry widows headed households; 'the guidwyff of Kilstaires', 'the guidwyff of Coclarachie', 'the guidwyff of Auchrydie', and a Janet Gordon, who was living with a daughter and no fewer than three servants, and was therefore in comfortable circumstances. 'Goodwife' is a courtesy title for the wife, or widow, of a laird. It is perhaps worth observing that the 'guidwyff of Coclarachie' was Elizabeth Duncan, widow of Gordon of Cochlarachie, an obdurate Catholic and ally of the Duke of Gordon – and thus part of the Catholic community in the Chanonry. Her son, William Gordon, was a doctor of medicine, and was probably the man of that name who was the Mediciner at King's.

The Middle Toun, like all Scots burghs in the seventeenth century, policed the morals of its citizenry, and was much concerned with order and discipline. Fornication was naturally frowned upon and severely dealt with, both by fines and by public humiliation. Nevertheless, 10 per cent of births were illegitimate in the parish in the late seventeenth century, and 40 per cent of brides were pregnant on their wedding day: well above the Scottish average. Drunkenness too was severely treated, but so also was harmless entertainment, such as 'pyping, fiddling, dansing trouble, bancatting nor other kyne of ryot' at weddings. That dancing at weddings, drinking and playing bowls on a Sunday, bringing dogs to church, and other offences against decency and gravity were so often inveighed against, shows clearly that the frivolously inclined went on offending, whatever the Kirk might say. An interesting form of misdemeanour, suggesting an obstinate adherence to traditions from before the Reformation, was lighting fires for Midsummer, which was banned in 1647, 1649 and 1650. It would seem that the ban was ineffective.

The Middle Toun was believed to have its share of witches: one Alexander Moultry was accused of raising the wind which blew down the stone crown from King's College steeple in 1633, and Jean Nimbrie was scolded for charming away a fever in 1681. Isoble Kelman was charged with killing a calf, and with having 'come over the watter of Don without ane boat' – witches, as was well known, being able to float – but the case collapsed for lack of evidence.

There was no hysteria, and none of the three were tortured, let alone burned. Common sense, and common humanity, were applied in all three cases.

Minor misdemeanors were punished by a fine or a session sitting in sackcloth on the stool of penitence, or sometimes both; the town also had a jail, a pair of stocks and a 'jougis'. This was an iron collar and chain, stapled to a market cross or a church door, and snapped round the neck of a malefactor who was thus left exposed to the jeers, or worse, of his fellow citizens. Sometimes his or her head was shaved first. Relative to the crimes, punishments were severe. A woman called Isobel Jemsone was convicted of stealing a shirt in 1608: she was formally disgraced at the market cross, the usual place for punishment, stripped to the waist, scourged through the town, and thrust into exile. Such punishments occurred often enough for the council to appoint an official scourge, Archbald Bischope, in 1636. Their enthusiasm for such forms of punishment may be linked with the fact that imprisoning wrongdoers cost money. Banishment was a serious threat, since any attempt to settle in another town would bring a visit from a Kirk official demanding to know if the individual possessed a testimonial of good character from his or her previous place of residence. Without such a report, the individual might well end up a homeless beggar.

Banishment and death were treated as ultimate remedies, with the trial sometimes used as a 'last warning'. A thief who broke into a tailor's after midnight in September 1652 and stole a variety of clothes was, like Isobel Jemsone, scourged throughout the town, and told that if she was ever seen there again she would be taken and drowned with no further ado. (There was no town gallows.) She might as easily have been executed at the time. A man called John Poak had some kind of grievance against Professor William Douglas: the whole issue was investigated, and Poak was told that if he subsequently swore at or bothered Douglas, he and his wife and family would be banished.

In 1613, a woman described as 'a cajoler of the students of King's College and abstracter of them from their studies' was banished from the town. Various attempts were made to prevent fraternisation between the students and the townspeople; as with the various actions taken against ungodly behaviour, the frequency of these orders suggests that lively social contact between the two groups did, in fact, occur. In 1605, brewsters were forbidden to 'givf any scholler ather meit or drink', and at the end of the same year, young men who were not householders were forbidden to play cards or dice, on pain of a fifteen-shilling fine. Unsurprisingly, after-hours drinking was also a problem for the authorities. No amount of legislation could stop the life of the college overspilling its bounds. Four academics, including the sub-principal and the mediciner, had manses outwith King's, and since the college was bursting at the seams, students lodged everywhere.

Old Aberdeen and the Civil Wars

The kirk session and town council records have surprisingly little to say about the civil war of the mid-seventeenth century. In 1638, the imposition of English forms of worship unleashed a furore of popular resistance which was embodied in the National Covenant. One Ayrshire divine, contemplating the hysteria, said, 'I think our people possessed with a bloody devill'. Meanwhile, the kirk in Old Aberdeen was more concerned about who was entitled to sit in each pew in St Machar's, and with taking up a collection to help ransom a luckless merchant's son enslaved by the Turks. This might have something to do with the fact that the local minister, who combined his charge with the rectorship of King's, was Alexander Scrogie, one of the 'Aberdeen Doctors' who were leading the opposition. Aberdeen, famously, was the only royal burgh which did not accept the Covenant. In the end, it was imposed by force. The bishop and chief bailie of Old Aberdeen reviewed the burgh's military forces, and found most of the

160 male inhabitants 'waik, febill and unarmed'. For the Covenanters, it was a walk-over. In the course of a day, 22 March 1639, King's College's staff and students were scattered, the college was locked up, and the bishop, Adam Bellenden, fled. A week later, Old Aberdeen had the doubtful honour of becoming the first town in Scotland to come under military occupation. About 2,000 Covenanters, twice its total population, appeared in arms and camped in and around the town, taking the opportunity to vandalise the bishop's palace. The Covenant was signed in the first week of April, under duress. It was perhaps with memories of this episode that the kirk session in the Old Town did, however, take note

The King Charles spire, seen from Cromwell Tower.

of the renewed Solemn League and Covenant, and insisted that it be signed. In January 1650, the principal of King's was asked to make a list of his students in order to ensure that those who had avoided signing it before should do so when asked for a second time.

In July 1644, the town observed the Scotland-wide general fast and humiliation for the success of the Scots army, which at that point was helping Oliver Cromwell to destroy the hopes of the royalists at Marston Moor near York. Then, late in the summer, the Kirk chronicles of illicit onion-selling, straying chickens, scolding wifies and misplaced rubbish are momentarily interrupted by the information that the town spent £300 Scots on thirty muskets along with their bandoliers, powder, match and bullets, 'for defence of the country againes the Ereis [Irish] rebels and wnnaturall countreymen'. Old Aberdeen was taxed for the outfitting of twelve foot soldiers and one horseman. The horseman cost £186 13s 4d to equip; the foot soldiers were not so expensive, but even so, each man needed 'two sarks, coat and breeks, hose and bonnet, bands and shoon [shoes]', as well as a sword, a musket or a pike, and for the musketeers, ammunition. The foot soldiers got six shillings a day; the horse-soldier would also have needed money to maintain his horse. Local chronicler John Spalding commented, 'sore was the poor people of the Old Town plucked and poinded to make up these soldiers' charges, wereas some of them had not [wherewith] to buy a loaf.'

The most famous of Scotland's royalist generals, the marquis of Montrose, was coming in force, with 1,500 Irish troops, to root the Covenanters out of Aberdeen. He broke their army in a brief and absolutely decisive battle.

Opposite. Bishop Elphinstone's arms adorn the sterling silver ceremonial mace of King's College, made in 1650 by Walter Melville.

Left. Inside the bars of the crown we find the Stuart arms of Great Britain: a typical gesture of defiant conservatism a year or more after the execution of Charles I and with no end to the English Commonwealth regime in sight.

Because the town had refused to surrender, for three days, his forces rampaged through it, looting, raping and murdering. The sources suggest that the Old Town got off relatively lightly, but it will have had its share of suffering. Spalding noted that two corpses ready for burial were carried through the burgh by 'wemen onlie' – absolutely contrary to Scots custom. Presumably the men dared not appear, and the women, with considerable courage, trusted that in the discharge of a universally respected solemn duty, they would be protected from rape or murder.

The burgh also heard of the sufferings of others. Penniless Protestant refugees were fleeing from Ireland from 1641 onwards with fearful tales of savage reprisals and 'no quarter'. Some of them fetched up even in distant Aberdeen, since we find the Kirk collecting money 'to be giuen to the Irish boyes that are at the scooles'. Despite Montrose's depredations, the burgh remained staunchly royalist: Charles II was crowned king on 1 January 1651, and in April, as he went south with a Scottish army to try and establish himself in England, a fast-day was held for him.

Paradoxically, Old Aberdeen did rather well out of the wars. The pride of the New Town was

GOD SAUE THE KING.

A Declaration of the Right Honourable JAMES
MARQVES of MONTROSE his Excellencie.

humbled by a huge burden of public debt, generated by military exactions and war damage. Royal burghs such as New Aberdeen also lost many of their exclusive economic privileges after 1672, making recovery even harder. Merchants moved to Old Aberdeen, where, as a burgh of barony and not a royal burgh, taxes were lower, and it thus became a more competitive place to do business. Property prices in the Old Town went through the roof, and the population more than doubled.

The general uncertainty following the death of Charles II and the accession of his Catholic brother was felt strongly in the Middle Town. Charles died early in February 1685, and in May of that year the town is found equipping four militia soldiers with new red coats and shoes, and sending them to a general rendezvous at

Turriff. The militiamen came out again for the Glorious Revolution in 1688, as did the town's modest collection of weaponry: nine firelock guns, two militia muskets, ten halberds, four swords and two pikes.

An Age of Reason and Unreason

St Machar's Kirk must have been a sad shell of a place by the time the great spire fell in 1688, demolishing much of the east end in its ruin. Though the roof was patched up, and a new east end cobbled together, the impulse towards glory at work among those who worshipped there was mostly bound up with their own aggrandisement. The Aberdeen Trades, and others of the citizenry who considered themselves a cut above

the rest, spent a good deal of money and political energy on building elaborate private desks and lofts, competing keenly with one another for prestigious positions. Only the poor and humble folk of the parish stood about in the nave, or sat on little stools they brought with them.

At the beginning of the eighteenth century, the population of Old Aberdeen was around 1,800. As the century wore on, the cityscape was transformed. Much of what we see in the High Street and Chanonry is eighteenth century: the graceful and dignified flat-fronted granite houses which now characterise the Old Town so strongly. Thatched roofs, so common in the seventeenth century, were steadily replaced with pantiles or slates.

The interesting question is where all the money for this refurbishment was coming from.

The events of the late seventeenth century brought a new prosperity to the town. Brick-making flourished down by the river, and a small sloop was kept busy bringing coals to the brick kilns. Many of these bricks were used in Old Aberdeen itself, which developed a distinctive habit of combining stone and brick in the same building.

Much of the money came from work done by women. The *Statistical Account* of 1791 states the major industry of Aberdeen was stocking-making. According to Alexander Skene, who published a *Succinct Survey* of both Aberdeens in 1685, the development of the trade was due to a single local hero, George Pyper, who encouraged women knitters to develop their skill: 'so ... that from five groats [1s 8d] the pair, he caused them work at such a fynness

One of many testaments to Old Aberdeen's eighteenth-century prosperity.

[fineness] that he hath given twenty shillings sterling and upward for the pair.' It was easier for women to find employment than men. Apart from knitting, the linen industry began to increase in importance as the century went on, and bleaching and thread-making were also women's work. Young men tended to emigrate and young women to stay put, while older women actually immigrated: 'the high probability of finding employment from some of the many manufactures carried on in this neighbourhood, induce many old women, and many of the widows and daughters of farmers and tradesmen, to leave the country to reside in this parish.' Stockings were exported in vast quantities, 219,360 pairs in 1743, and nearly a million pairs just fifty years later, mostly to Holland; considerable fortunes were made by the men who organised the trade.

The eighteenth century was a great era for clubs and societies, and saw the creation of a new forum for the meeting of town and gown. King's professor Thomas Reid was instrumental in the development of a philosophical society, known to those who frequented it as the Wise Club, in 1758. For fifteen years, academics and townsmen came together fortnightly to debate new ideas. James Beattie, nationally famous poet and philosopher, was another member.

Salmon fishing on the Don continued to be lucrative and important, and King's contributed to its success when Dr John Gregory (a member of a brilliant academic dynasty of mathematicians and doctors) destroyed an encroaching

Another instance of Old Aberdeen's distinctive habit of combining stone and brick in the same building.

80

sandbank and created a much-wanted deep channel by building a carefully sited stone bulwark: this caused the river to wash away the sand instead of adding to it, thus showing how the abstract knowledge cultivated in the college could also have practical applications.

An aspect of national politics which was very strongly felt in Old Aberdeen was the pro-Stuart loyalism which erupted after the death of Queen Anne. The bells of St Machar's were rung to celebrate the arrival at London of the first Hanoverian king, George I, in 1714, but most Aberdonians would rather have rung them for Anne's brother, James VIII, the Old Pretender. On 10 August 1714, nine days after Anne's death, a group of men including Jon Urquhart, George Cuming, William Gordon and Patrick Forbes, and 'sevll women' – and/or men 'under the disguise of womens apparrell' – were accused of proclaiming James VIII king in New Aberdeen and singing 'Lett the King enjoy his owne againe' (a popular loyalist song of the civil-war period), accompanied by 'two viollers'. Ten months later, Alexander Gordon the younger of Auchlyne, hearing that some men were going to proclaim the Old Pretender again, attacked them with the assistance of his servant, wounding nine. It was to the sound of a drum, played – against his will, he later claimed – by William Walker, that the Old Pretender was proclaimed in Old Aberdeen in 1715 by Robert Warrander, a bursar of King's

James Francis Edward Stuart, known to his enemies as the Old Pretender, to his friends as King James VIII and III. This portrait after Alexis Simon Belle would have been owned by a wealthy supporter. Poorer Jacobites showed their allegiance with slogans, mottos and portraits engraved on a variety of commonplace objects, especially drinking vessels.

Left. After fighting at the battle of Sherrifmuir in his teens, James Keith rose to senior command rank in the Spanish and Russian armies in turn, but claimed he was discriminated against by the former because he was a Protestant and by the latter because he was a foreigner. Of Lutheran Prussia he made no such complaints, and he died in action in 1758, one of Frederick the Great's field marshals. Not all Jacobites were as well born or as successful, but Keith's story reflects, in an extreme form, the vagaries of the military exile experience. Portrait by Alexis Simon Belle, 1724.

College. Warrander was accompanied by a number of his fellow students, probably including Patrick Ogilby, John Ogilby, William Moir, Angus Sage, Patrick Douglas, William Ord, and Kenneth McKenzie. For generations, King's College would remain broadly supportive of the Jacobite cause (see box, p.84): a small group of undergraduates were even disciplined for burning a picture of 'the Duke of Brunswick', as they termed George I. At the Forty-five, the town was divided between enthusiastic Jacobites such as John Gordon of Glenbucket, and pro-Hanoverians. When the battle of Culloden put paid to Jacobite hopes, the St Machar's kirk session proclaimed a day of thanksgiving.

Though the Covenanters of the seventeenth century had done all they could to enforce religious conformity upon Aberdeen, it is clear that they had not been particularly successful.

Catholics continued to be discreetly buried in the graveyard of Snow Kirk, and King's resisted any attempt to enquire into this state of affairs. Marriages were not always conducted by the minister, as they should have been: the author of the *Statistical Account* complains that 'loose and disorderly persons' had in effect created a form of civil marriage. Such couples would move in together, and then go before the magistrate and pay a fine, thereafter referring to him 'as the celebrator of the marriage'. The fine was supposed to be high enough to prevent such behaviour, but magistrates connived by reducing it to half a guinea, five shillings, or even less. Thus Catholics and Episcopalians could discreetly get married before a priest of their own faith, and make the union legal by squaring it with the secular authorities, circumventing the Kirk entirely.

Opposite right. Captain Roy's map of Old Aberdeen in the mid-eighteenth century.

Left. This gilded copper gorget was worn around the neck of professor the Rev. Gilbert Gerard, major-commandant of the Old Aberdeen Volunteers in 1802. Technically armour, its only real value was as a symbol of rank.

Dr Johnson in Old Aberdeen

Samuel Johnson and his faithful biographer, James Boswell, passed through Aberdeen in the course of their Scottish tour of 1773. Johnson was by then celebrated for his great English dictionary, and also for his ready wit and immense enjoyment of arguments, which he much preferred to win. When he came to Aberdeen, he was pleased and surprised to get a letter from a very old friend, Sir Alexander Gordon, 'whom I had formerly known in London, and after a cessation of all intercourse for near twenty years met here professor of physic [medicine] in the King's College. Such unexpected renewals of acquaintance may be numbered among the most pleasing incidents of life.'

His friendship with Gordon threw open the doors of Old Aberdeen to Johnson.

Though Johnson's combative reputation had gone before him, the other professors were delighted to meet this distinguished visitor; or it might be more accurate to say that they all wanted to be able to say afterwards that they had met him. Dr Gordon held a dinner for Johnson to which all his colleagues came, but the ever-observant Boswell noticed that 'the professors seemed afraid to speak', anxious to avoid drawing his fire. Johnson, rather disappointed, got more enjoyment from walking after dinner in Gordon's garden. Boswell (alone) attests to the existence of a formal baroque garden in Old Aberdeen: 'we sauntered after dinner in Sir Alexander's garden, and saw his little grotto, which is hung with pieces of poetry written in a fair hand. It was agreeable to observe the contentment and kindness of this quiet, benevolent man.' Many seventeenth- and

Jacobitism

The Jacobite rebellions are enormously important to the story of Old Aberdeen. Always intensely conservative in its leanings, the burgh on the whole found the 'Glorious Revolution' unacceptable because it was change from the old ways – quite apart from the new issues which it spawned.

These were substantial. The groundswell of pro-Stuart loyalism which set in after the execution of Charles I in 1649 and induced the Scots to offer the crown of Scotland to Charles II in 1651, a good ten years before his Restoration to the English throne, set a Scottish pattern of loyalty to the Stuarts which lasted into the eighteenth century. The Presbyterians who crowned the youthful Charles II had a very poor opinion of him as a person, but nonetheless, they had a firm conviction that he was and must remain the true king of Scots.

Charles II was cynical, clever, and in many respects, good at his job. Unfortunately, though his subjects enjoyed the dubious honour of supporting a dozen royal bastards, he had no legitimate offspring. His heir was therefore his younger brother James, and like their father Charles I, James was both stupid and obstinate. Charles II was privately sympathetic to Catholicism, and died in that faith, but had more sense than to flaunt it in public. James VII (II of England), on the other hand, converted publicly, and married a staunchly Catholic wife, Mary of Modena, to whom he was nevertheless compulsively unfaithful – leading Charles, with characteristic detachment, to observe, 'My brother will lose his kingdom by his bigotry, and his soul for a lot of ugly trollops.' James's attempts to create a religiously plural society were vehemently resisted by the English. The very genuine fears created by his policies were mitigated only by the comforting thought that the problems he was creating were finite. He was elderly, his children by his Catholic wife all died shortly after their births, and his two daughters by an earlier, Protestant, wife were both themselves staunch Protestants.

Then, in June 1688, Mary of Modena gave birth to a healthy-looking son. By the end of that year, with the spectre of a Catholic succession looming, James had been forced into exile in France, and his eldest daughter Mary, supported by her husband William of Orange and his army, was Queen of England. Scarcely a shot had been fired but resistance to the Revolution Settlement, armed as well as passive, would continue for decades.

For the constitutionally minded, William's invasion and assumption of the throne were profoundly dismaying. Was not the Lord's Anointed the Lord's Anointed until he died? Not a few loyal subjects, in England and Ireland as well as in Scotland, thought so, and therefore felt morally bound by their oaths of loyalty. James's policies were if anything even less loved north of the border than they were in England, but until he actually died, to many, he was still the monarch, and William and Mary were not. From this point onwards, the supporters of James and his descendants were called Jacobites, from *Jacobus,* the Latin form of James's name that appeared on the coinage and other official matter.

One group who suffered particularly were Scottish Episcopalians. Clerics in the Church of England were required to take an oath of loyalty to William and Mary, and significant numbers refused to do so. They were deprived of their livings and became a sort of shadow church. In Scotland the same requirement resulted in the entire body of bishops refusing the oath in 1689. They were therefore ousted en masse, and the Presbyterian Kirk became the established Church of Scotland in their place. This especially affected Aberdeenshire, where there was far less attachment to the Kirk than in the south of the country. When Daniel Defoe (*c.*1660–1731) visited the city during his Scottish tour, he observed correctly that the 'abundance of the people are still episcopal in their opinion'.

Old Aberdeen did not lead resistance to the proclamation of William and Mary in the way that it had led resistance to the National Covenant of 1638. But it is easy to see why. The government quartered in Aberdeen a pro-William army under a general with no local loyalties, Hugh Mackay of Scourie, over the winter of 1688–89, so while the town's feelings were almost certainly pro-James, they did not stretch as far as courting martyrdom for his cause. Even so, the response of both the university and the burgh to the new régime could at best be described as lukewarm.

The next problem facing the Stuart loyalists was the death of Queen Anne. William and Mary had no children, but anyone who had been able to square the Williamite succession with his or her conscience could not, in reason, object to the accession of her younger sister Anne as her successor. Anne's life was dominated by the personal and national tragedy of her desperate attempts to produce an heir. She endured eighteen pregnancies, twelve of which resulted in a stillborn child. Another three of her babies died the day they were born, while two made it past their second birthday, but not to their third. One fragile boy-child lived to the age of eleven, but also predeceased her. Thus when the unfortunate queen finally died in 1714, another agonising political dilemma presented itself. Unfortunately, the procreative abilities of the Stuarts had finally asserted themselves in the most inconvenient fashion. James Francis Edward Stuart, whose arrival as a baby had precipitated his father's loss of his throne, was alive and well, the legitimate son and heir of a crowned and anointed king of England and Scotland. He was also a Catholic, and pro-French to the point of being in effect a French army general. The alternative to James Francis – in the sense of being a Protestant, male relative of the house of Stuart – was something of an out-cousin, son of the youngest daughter of Charles I's sister. His father was the duke of Braunschweig-Lüneburg, his name was Georg, and he spoke no English. But at least he was a Protestant.

The strength of the case for James Francis plus the weakness of the case for Georg made it almost inevitable that the Jacobites would challenge the latter for power. George I was crowned on 20 October 1714, and on 22 December 1715 James Francis Edward, or James VIII, finally set foot in Scotland. By the time he arrived, the armed rebellion in his name, later known as the Fifteen, had been raging since the summer. It was not the first or the last armed Jacobite uprising, but it came the closest to success as it was identified with opposition to the increasingly unpopular 1707 Act of Union. The political party in England and Wales then known as the Tories was also seen, rightly or wrongly, as being sympathetic to the Fifteen. Even so, armed support for the Stuart king in the wealthy and powerful south of England was negligible, and more than half of James's many soldiers were Scottish Episcopalians.

Their efforts terrified the Hanoverian élite but were abortive, meeting solid resistance as they headed southward. James had been recognised as king by France, Spain, the Papal States and his mother's homeland of Modena; he might have hoped, therefore, that France at least would offer him significant military and other support, but this did not materialise. Part of the reason for this was that Louis XIV died in the summer of 1715 and was succeeded by a five-year-old great-grandson.

A second serious attempt on the throne, led by James Francis's son Charles Edward ('Bonny Prince Charlie') in 1745–46 covered more territory with fewer troops: defeating the government forces outright at Prestonpans, gaining support in Manchester where a Jacobite regiment was formed, and penetrating England as far as Derby. It was still ultimately unsuccessful. By far the most numerous and conspicuous of Charles's supporters were Highland clans (though even in the Highlands, by no means all the clans 'came out' for him). This was particularly unfortunate since the inhabitants of England and the more settled regions of Scotland by and large regarded the clansmen as lawless and brutally violent robbers. As such, they were less than persuasive politically. Nevertheless, large numbers of Episcopalians, from the Lowlands as well as the Highlands, were only able to come to terms with the de facto Williamite-Hanoverian monarchy in 1766. In that year, James VIII (III of England) died, and no crowned head of state recognised Charlie as 'Charles III', despite his own best efforts. Tired of wars and persecution that had lasted more than seventy years, the Jacobites needed to lay their Stuart loyalty aside – but with honour. The death of James VIII and the non-recognition of his son gave them their moment.

Incidentally, this serves somewhat to explain one of the great paradoxes of Scottish–American identity: how the same families and, indeed, individuals could have fought against George II in 1745, but for George III in 1776.

A disappointed alcoholic, Charles Edward Stuart followed his father to the grave in 1788. But for some the Jacobite quarrel did not entirely die until his younger brother, Henry Benedict – intelligent, discreetly homosexual and a Catholic priest – met a peaceful end in his villa at Frascati in 1807.

For a tiny number of true believers, it has never ended.

Old Aberdeen as it appeared at the time of Dr Johnson's visit.

eighteenth-century gardens were laid out to provoke a particular sequence of thought and decked with inscriptions, while grottos in particular had been made popular by Alexander Pope earlier in the eighteenth century. Johnson found the excursion tiring, essentially because Dr Gordon was so anxious to entertain him that he made the classic mistake of doing far too much and not giving his guest a moment's peace.

All the same, Johnson found Old Aberdeen both interesting and picturesque, and was one of many to note the importance of stocking-making to the economy of the burgh. He was also impressed by King's, whose 'first president [Hector Boece] may be justly reverenced as one of the revivers of elegant learning'.

Boswell and Johnson were going on to a tour of the Hebrides, and were therefore gratified to find that Professor Macleod of King's was the brother-in-law of the laird of Coll (in the Inner Hebrides), and able to give them an introduction. The McLeans of Coll were much involved with Old Aberdeen. In 1771, two years before Boswell and Johnson's visit, the McLeans had laid the foundation stone of a splendid new town house, which is still standing at 81 High Street. The family were prominent in Old Aberdeen affairs, and Hugh McLean was chief magistrate in Old Aberdeen in the late eighteenth century.

Old Aberdeen and Early America

Old Aberdeen contributed to the making of America in four significant areas: religion, education, scientific study, and the development of Carolina. The graveyard of St Peter's in the Spital holds the grave of John Skinner, one of the three Scottish bishops who consecrated Bishop Samuel Seabury, the first Episcopalian bishop in the Americas. The problem that an independent America raised for the Church of England was that its bishops were forbidden by law to consecrate anyone who would not take an oath of allegiance to the British Crown. Seabury therefore turned to the Scottish Episcopal Church which, though doctrinally very similar, had no connection with government. After the deposition of James II and VII in 1688, the Scottish bishops refused to swear an oath of allegiance to William III; Presbyterian church government was thus re-established in the Church of Scotland, and those who would not accept the new king – the 'non-jurors' – were excluded from any share in it. Since they were not part of the establishment, the Scottish bishops were accordingly free to consecrate an American bishop without political complications. In Aberdeen, on 14 November 1784, Samuel Seabury was consecrated to the episcopate by the bishop and the bishop

The major elements of King's College's eighteenth-century skyline can still be seen. A modern anemometer has replaced Cromwell Tower's weathercock but elements of a Georgian observatory remain. From left to right: Luthuli House, the Crown Tower, the King Charles spire and Cromwell Tower.

Right and opposite. De Bry illustrations from A Wonderful and Faithful Narration of the Goods and Religion of the Inhabitants of Virginia.

coadjutor of Aberdeen and the bishop of Ross and Caithness.

Other Scottish Episcopalians went to minister in America: one such was James Stuart, rector of Prince George parish, Winyaw (now part of Georgetown District), South Carolina. Though his ancestry is not known, he must have had strong connections with Aberdeenshire, since he bequeathed £2,000 in 3 per cent consols for the support of bursars, and £1,200 to support the education of young men named Stuart or Simpson at Fordyce and Banff academies, and then, in 1809, at Marischal and King's.

A later resident of Prince George parish, Dr Philip Tidyman (1776–1850) was one of the most intellectually distinguished citizens of nineteenth-century Charleston. He was the first American, in 1800, to receive an MD from the University of Göttingen, then one of the greatest universities of the world. His dissertation was *Commentatio inauguralis de Oryza Sativa* – that is to say, *On Rice*, a highly practical study since rice was the great industry of Carolina, and his plantation, which bears the name of Tidyman's Marsh, was well adapted to rice cultivation. Tidyman wrote on medical issues and was a patron of art. He commissioned two pictures from Thomas Sully, the portrait painter of Philadelphia, and miniatures of his wife and daughter from Walter Robertson. But he came, in fact, from Old Aberdeen, and died there. A memorial was raised to him in the transept of St Machar, noting that he was 'connected by descent with this country which had been endeared to him by the recollections of early youth'. He was revisiting the town after an absence of fifty-two years when he died.

Old Aberdeen's connections with Charleston go well back into the seventeenth century. James Fraser (1645–1731), educated at King's College, Aberdeen, became tutor to one of Charles II's several illegitimate sons in the mid-1660s and thereafter held various posts under royal patronage. Many letters to and from Fraser survive at King's, including a manuscript account of Carolina, endorsed in Fraser's own hand as 'a Letter giving an account of Carolina in the West Indies written by an ingenious French gentleman to Mr Fraser, Anno 1691'. Its author, Jean Boyd, seems, on the evidence of another letter in the same bundle, to have been a cousin of Fraser's whose family had settled in France. Boyd was an assemblyman in Carolina, where he lived for some time. His writings and drawings describe Native Americans and the building of Charleston, as well as the flora and fauna of 'this most beautiful country in the world', and include the first surviving representation of Charleston on its present site.

The Ogilvie family of Auchiries also tried their luck in Carolina. Having been drawn into the 1745 Jacobite rebellion, the Ogilvies were 'lucky to escape alive with property intact', and three brothers went to Carolina, where Charles Ogilvie was sufficiently successful to bring his nephew George to America to assist him. George Ogilvie wrote from Myrtle Grove Plantation, Colleton County, in June 1774: 'I slept last night for the first time in my life at least four miles distant from any white person like the Tyrant of some Asiatick Isle the only free man in an Island of Slaves.' Later in the same letter, he describes

eating broiled chicken and wild cherries in a temperature of ninety-two degrees, with a thunderstorm coming. He became a dedicated and effective planter, with a strong sense of his responsibilities towards his slaves. But the Ogilvies remained loyal to the British Crown at the Revolution, despite their Jacobite heritage. George had to leave Carolina in haste; in a letter of 25 April he movingly records his sorrow and anxiety about his slaves:

In this Land of Nominal freedom and actual Slavery, Self-Love suggested that by aleviating the too common weight of the chain, I might in some degree justify the keeping my fellow beings in bondage . . . for these three years past, besides as much corn as they can use, I have allowed them flesh meat, twice or thrice every week or even oftener, when hard work'd, & notwithstanding the enormous advance in the price of Clothing, have even made a small addition to the usual allowance – whilst many of the Richest men here have not clothed their negroes for two or even three years. But now I fear they must all be subjected to the most humiliating circumstance of human nature, that of being sold like the Brutes that Perish; and when deprived of the little indulgences I allowed them, will they not have reason to curse me for having taught them wants that they might else have never known?

A friend of the Ogilvies who was similarly born and educated in Aberdeen but emigrated to Carolina was Dr Alexander Garden (1730–91).

Garden was the first systematic botanist of the American South, the man after whom the gardenia is named, and a correspondent of Linnaeus. His correspondence with the Ogilvies includes a nostalgic description, written in 1789, of his beloved gardens at Otranto in Berkeley County, South Carolina, which he had been forced to abandon. It was one of the very first botanical pleasure-gardens ever made in the New World, for which he had used only native plants.

These collections of letters and other material from these three exceptionally lively and observant men reveal how much they contributed to Carolina life, in terms of real commitment, enthusiasm, and love for their adopted country. They also tell of impending catastrophe and personal tragedy, escape via the Caribbean, and American-exile life in London. George Ogilvie wrote broken-heartedly from London: 'I am restored to my native land stripd almost naked of Property and dependent, in my old age, upon the Justice of a Nation that seems to have lost every Idea of that Virtue, as well as its Honor.' But there is also a happier epilogue. A younger generation of Ogilvies and Gardens returned to Carolina to become American citizens.

Old Aberdeen boasts a strong connection to the ornithology as well as the botany of America. One of the greatest of all ornithological works, John James Audubon's *Birds of America* owes much to Aberdeen ornithologist William MacGillivray (1796–1852). MacGillivray played a substantial part in the writing of the 'Ornithological Biographies' which accompanied Audubon's wonderful colour plates, and Audubon commemorated his collaborator in the naming of two American birds, both illustrated in his magnum opus: 'MacGillivray's Ground Warbler' and 'MacGillivray's Shore Finch'. MacGillivray later became professor of natural history at Aberdeen, so his copious ornithological notes, interspersed with beautifully observed records of his field expeditions in northern Scotland, and even some of the actual bird skins from which Audubon worked, came to King's and can still be seen there.

Cosmo Alexander, Jacobite painter of the Old Aberdeen Sibyls, also worked in America late in his career. In Rhode Island in 1769, he took on as a pupil Gilbert Stuart, son of a local Scottish immigrant snuff-miller. Stuart went on to a prolific painting career that would include arguably the most famous portrait from life of President George Washington.

One of the most significant Aberdonian interventions in the developing intellectual culture of eighteenth-century America was that of Dr William Smith (1727–1803), who was born in Aberdeen and educated at King's. He emigrated to America in 1751, and his 1753 essay, *A General Idea of the College of Mirania*, impressed Benjamin Franklin so much that Smith was appointed to teach logic and natural philosophy at the College of Philadelphia. Smith subsequently served as first provost there. Although he was himself an Episcopal clergyman, during his directorship (which ended before the college became the University of the State of Pennsylvania in 1779), he encouraged students of all faiths to enrol, and held that true religion was to be learned from truthful and ethical teaching. His intellectual distinction was marked by his receipt of three honorary doctorates: from King's College, Aberdeen; the University of Oxford; and Trinity College, Dublin. He died in 1803, just before his conse-

cration as first Episcopalian bishop of Maryland. His continued remembrance of Aberdeen is suggested by his gift of his own book, *Discourses on Public Occasions in America*, to the library of King's, and also by a copy of the *Transactions of the American Philosophical Society* (volume 1, Philadelphia, 1771), which has the fascinating inscription: 'The American Philosophical Society held at Philadelphia humbly desires to cooperate with the University of Aberdeen, in their laudable Endeavours for the Advancement of useful Knowledge.' It is further inscribed, 'Dr Smith begs that Dr Franklin would direct this copy to Dr John Chalmers, Principal, for the library of King's College, Old Aberdeen, in which place Dr Smith had his Education.'

Another Episcopalian, Alexander Murray, also remembered his former home from Philadelphia. Having graduated MA from King's in 1746, he became an Anglican missionary at Reading, Pennsylvania. He died in Philadelphia in 1793, and by his will established the Murray lectureships: a series of winter-Sunday lectures set up in King's College Chapel to save students and staff from attending their parish services at St Machar's in poor weather. It seems he had never forgotten the physical rigours of student life in Old Aberdeen.

The King's College That Almost Was

James Byres, son of the Jacobite and Catholic Patrick Byres of Tonley, was taken to the Continent by his parents when they fled Scotland after the failed rising of 1745. By 1758, Byres was studying painting in Rome, but by 1768 he had been elected to the Roman artists' guild, the

John Adam, the eldest son of William Adam, drew this redesign for the west front of King's College in about 1780.

Accademia di San Luca, as an architect. He was a friend of Giovanni Battista Piranesi (1720–78) and from the early 1760s one of the leading figures in the aesthetic world of Rome as experienced by the 'grand tourist'. Byres acted as an antiquarian guide, most notably to the historian Edward Gibbon, but also as an agent introducing potential patrons to painters, as an art dealer handling such fine paintings as Poussin's *Seven Sacraments* (now in the National Gallery of Scotland) and such notable objects as the Portland Vase now in the British Museum. In Rome he lived in some state in the Strada Paolina with a household that included at various times his parents and nephew and his partner Christopher Norton (*c.*1740–99) as well as his fellow painter and antiquary Colin Morison. Byres returned to Scotland in 1790 and lived out a long retirement on his Aberdeenshire estates. Throughout his career he made fine architectural designs, few of which were executed, with the exception of the superb classical mausoleum which he designed for his neighbour Miss Fraser of Castle Fraser.

Five drawings for a rebuilding of King's College, Aberdeen, in the manner of a Roman palace, were undertaken by Byres in 1767. The main influence is Borromini's: his buildings for

C

the University of Rome, the *Sapienza*, and his library for the oratorians at the Chiesa Nuova. Byres's plan would have clothed the inner quadrangle at King's with two-storey cloisters and would have concealed the crown spire behind a palace front, with a block advancing to the street-line of the High Street. One of the sections through Byres's projected front block indicates a library room looking inward to the courtyard, triple height, with two ranges of galleries, ornamented with a statue of Atlas bearing the world. A large and magnificent room with a dome is allowed for a museum, on the scale of the *Tribuna* of the Uffizi in Florence.

Byres's associate Colin Morison, a graduate of Marischal College, intended his substantial collection of 300 Italian paintings 'of all the great Italian masters, from the invention of oil-painting down to the perfection of the art by Raphael' to come to King's College. Had this happened, it would have formed one of the earliest public picture galleries in Britain, contemporary with the Dulwich Gallery. After his death in 1810, Morison's collection was seized by the French as enemy property and dispersed. His and Byres's ambitions for Old Aberdeen may, however, explain the sumptuous museum room which is at the centre of these plans.

Above and overleaf. These drawings for a rebuilding of King's College in the manner of a Roman palace were undertaken by James Byres in 1767. The designs would have concealed the crown spire behind the palace front.

93

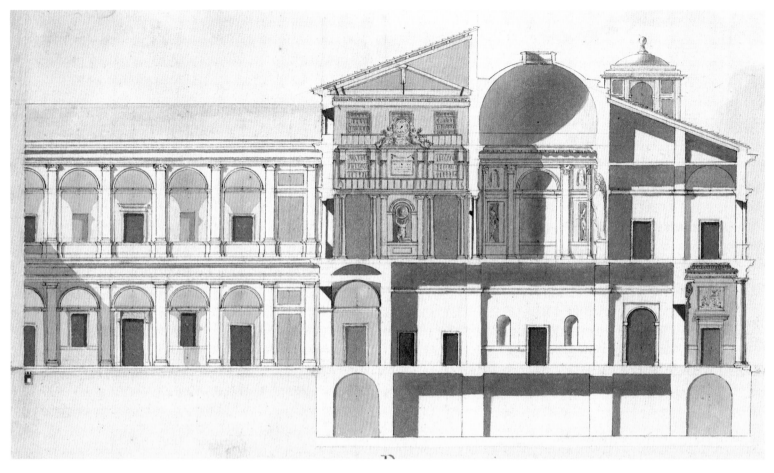

'Gibberie Wallie'

An Old Aberdeen resident, John Forbes, was out shooting hares in the winter of 1721 when he happened to notice a spring which arose just south of the Powis Burn on Little Firhill. He was a sufferer from bladder stones, an agonisingly painful and quite common complaint among the early-modern élite, possibly due to their preference for a diet extensively based on meat. Hence there was a good deal of interest in possible remedies short of surgery, the solution of last resort in those days before anaesthesia or antibiotics. Forbes happened to be thirsty, drank

some of the water and immediately observed that he felt a significant easing of his discomfort. He drank some more, and when the water had worked through his system, he managed to pass a quantity of gravel and small bladder stones. Therafter, he swore by the water, and resorted to it whenever the trouble returned. By the early 1750s, the spring is clearly identified as 'Mineral Springs' on Andrew Logie's plan, and defined as 'A Well' – suggesting that the water source had been isolated and made more usable – in Captain Taylor's plan of 1773. A quarter century later, it was further improved by public subscription, and the road to Firhill (a footpath which ran alongside the Powis Burn from beside the Red Lion Inn on the Spital) also received attention. It was duly written up in 1800 by Dr J. Taylor, a fellow of the Royal College of Physicians of Edinburgh, who indicated that it had been fitted up in quite a sophisticated way: 'the well has been lately inclosed with a stone wall; the water runs from a brass spout, into a stone bason . . . at the sole expense of a few public-spirited Gentlemen.' Two long arms of stone benching extended to either side of the actual source, and this seating had to be supplemented by wooden seats as the spring became better and better known.

New Aberdeen had long had a mineral well, hailed by William Barclay in 1615 in a long poem, *Callirhoe, commonly called the Well of Spa*. Now Old Aberdeen had one of its own and Dr Taylor was minded to make the most of it. He burst only briefly into verse ('Thou best of fountains, by all bounteous Heaven'), but his description of the well in its setting can fairly be described as lyrical:

> *The appearance of our well is somewhat romantic, environed with pleasure-grounds, a grove, an hermitage, and the lofty tower of King's College, highly ornamented with a stately imperial crown. On the other hand, two high pyramids, of a singular structure, appear; they belong to the church of Saint Machar, being the remains of an ancient cathedral, – in a word, the whole vicinity may be said to consummate a perfect symmetry of the agreeable and beautiful.*

Taylor argued that the Firhill Well was actually better than the Spa Well of New Aberdeen for two reasons: first, that it was rather more heavily mineralised, and second, that the moderate amount of healthy exercise needed to reach it via the footpath was a benefit in itself. A whole series of sufferers from bladder conditions found the water helped them, and it also relieved asthma, stomach pains, and at least one sufferer from sore eyes.

The popularity of the well was increased from 1815 to 1830 by an additional inducement, the gingerbread sold by a formidable old lady called Baubie Courage (also apparently known as Mrs Davidson). She did not make it, but bought it from Robert Murray, baker of Castle Street in New Aberdeen. Since the medicinal water, like that of all so-called chalybeate springs, tasted repulsive, she found that she drove a good trade, and the Firhill Well became known as 'Gibberie [Gingerbread] Wallie', in accordance with the general Aberdeenshire use of '-ie' as an affectionate diminutive. Gingerbread became so closely associated with the experience of visiting the spring that the name Gibberie Wallie completely superseded the more dignified Firhill Well over the years.

Unfortunately, Mrs Courage's avocation led to altercations with the Rev. Patrick Forbes, King's humanist and minister of St Machar's, who lived in Humanity Manse (19 College Bounds), the garden of which was immediately adjacent to the well. The Wallie had become a favoured courting spot for local youngsters, whose only day off was a Sunday. More gibberie was sold on a Sunday than on any other day, and doubtless there was also a certain amount of larking about, noise, and disturbance. Professors and teenagers have seldom seen eye to eye, but this was worse in that Forbes deeply disapproved of Sabbath-breaking. He threatened Courage with excommunication. However, things had moved on since the seventeenth century; this last weapon of the Kirk proved ineffective, and he got a stream of abuse for his pains.

Baubie Courage died at the age of eighty in 1830, but the gibberie continued, and another woman assumed the white apron and wicker basket. Children and young people continued to favour the Wallie as a playground, not least because they were sure of finding the gibberie wifie at her post. The actual spring ran dry in the 1860s, probably because the sand of the Little Firhill was gradually removed in the course of the decade for builders' use, but Katherine Trail was still visiting the well a decade later, and enjoying the gingerbread.*

Victorian Twilight

The decline of industry in Old Aberdeen, combined with the increasing size of the university, ensured that more and more of the community revolved around King's. The professors had always been important people in the town, and they became even more so. The burgh became something of a backwater, quaint and self-sufficient. Katherine Trail, looking back to a childhood in the 1870s, commented:

I am most struck with the curious isolation in which we used to live in Old Aberdeen. We were absolutely self-contained – that is to say, all our wants, both spiritual and corporal, were well looked after without any intervention

Right. The banks of the Don at Balgownie, about 1870, showing a variety of local pastimes and occupations.

Opposite. Balgownie village.

* In the 1930s, the council decided to develop the area as a sports ground, and in 1937 moved the wellhead with its benching forty yards south-west, to the edge of the St Machar Bowling Green. This was to make room for a new road which was never in fact built.

Pottery at Seaton

Pottery was made at Clayhills in New Aberdeen from the mid-thirteenth century onwards, and it is perfectly possible that the clay seam to the west of Old Aberdeen was discovered and put to good use in the Middle Ages. Bricks were made on the links at Seaton in Old Aberdeen from at least the mid-eighteenth century by Alexander Annand & Company. Annand's business went on the market in 1773, when it was described as seven acres on the east side of Old Aberdeen, on the west of the 'tile burn' and including clay pits and ground, house, office, barn, stable, kiln, mill and utensils. The works made bricks and tiles, chimney cans and other ceramic building materials.

In 1868 a more ambitious ceramics business was inaugurated at Seaton, producing both utility and decorative items. Aimed in their own time at a rather humble client base, these are now much sought after. In its first phase of life, up to 1903, the pottery's most characteristic products were dabbed food-storage barrels, butter tubs and cheese bells in rich greens, blues and browns, and a kind of agate ware, produced by throwing three different-coloured clays together.

Another characteristic product was large bowls: bread pancheons and the wide dishes in which milk was left to let the cream rise to the top boldly hand-decorated with the name of the owner and a date. Such pieces were made for weddings, or other momentous occasions in the life of a household. Beyond the sense that these different types of pottery were made there, very few pieces were stamped with a maker's mark and it is therefore often difficult to definitely assign objects to Seaton.

Seaton Pottery was founded by a master potter from Lanarkshire called Thomas Gavin, together with James Ritchie. It was sufficiently prosperous to give work to eight people: three men, three boys and two girls. In the 1890s, John and Hugh Gavin took over from their father, but the venture came to an end in 1903.

In the same year the plant and equipment were bought by a local florist, Ben Reid & Company Ltd, who employed two potters from Derbyshire called Clarke and Smith to work it for them. They converted the business into an art pottery and installed new plant. Stamped pieces which survive from this period are mainly vases with the impressed mark: CLARKE & SMITH/SEATON POTTERY/ABERDEEN in an oval. After less than two years in Aberdeen, they gave up and Seaton Pottery was again on the brink of closure.

When Clarke and Smith left in 1905, a potter had not owned it since 1899. Until 1904, Arthur Mills had worked with his two brothers and father at the pottery of Joseph Bourne & Son, Denby, Derbyshire. During the Clarke and Smith period, Arthur came to Aberdeen with his family to work as a pottery thrower, and in October 1905 he took over the running of Seaton Pottery. His third son, Ivor, joined him there in 1915 and the company became known as A. Mills & Son. Ivor took over running the works in 1927 when his father became ill. Until 1946, when mechanisation came in the form of two brand-new moulding machines, all the flowerpots were hand-made on one of just three throwing wheels. However, the introduction of plastic flowerpots, as well as the council's desire to acquire the land for housing and recreational use, eventually brought an end to it, and the pottery closed for good in 1964.

This Seaton Pottery bowl, probably made as a wedding present, is dated 1862 and decorated with an eclectic variety of nautical, royal, natural and personal emblems.

This simpler Seaton cream bowl was hand-made for a Mrs Yule in 1888, using a technique known as 'sgrafitto'.

from the neighbouring city. We had our churches and our schools, and our own doctors . . . our own butcher, baker and grocer, a vegetable shop for those whose gardens did not give them all they required, and we even had a shop for haberdashery and millinery. We had a post office, which was also the chemist's shop.

The Old Town's first brewery had been chartered by Bishop Elphinstone in 1504. Gilbert Plot, his wife and their heirs were allowed to run it for an annual rent of two merks (£1 6s 8d), the money to be used for masses for the soul of Henry Lychton (bishop of Aberdeen 1422–40). Into modern times the burgh boasted a good few brewsters, some of them women. It was a common occupation for widows, as well as for wives who needed to bring extra income to their families. The council did its best to ensure that the water which entered the town was clean, and beer-making benefited accordingly. Later brewing was on a larger scale, and was the last industry to survive in the town, though nearby Seaton Pottery (see box, p.98) would soldier on until the 1960s. In 1811, William Kennedy noted that 'Old Aberdeen never was a place of commerce, and the only branch of manufacture carried on in it, at present, is an extensive brewery, which supplies the citizens and neighbourhood with beer, ale and porter . . . it has been conducted, for several years by an established company.' There were three breweries then operating in Old Machar parish, but of these only Smith, Irvine & Company was located in Old Aberdeen proper.

Brewing flourished through the nineteenth century, perhaps unsurprisingly given the number of thirsty students. It also acquired a royal seal of approval. Trail recalled that one brewery

did a very big business, sending its carts all over the countryside. It was a great sight when a cart laden with barrels of beer, drawn by two splendid, beautifully groomed horses, their harness polished to the last degree of shine, set out for Balmoral with beer for Queen Victoria's household ... it was a two days' journey to Balmoral, and two days home again[.]

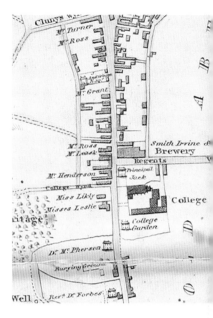

Its owner, Mr Thomson, had a passion for horses, so the dray horses were always magnificently turned out. He lived opposite the brewery in the house then called Powis Lodge.

After the Smith Irvine brewery closed, its buildings, which date from the late eighteenth or early nineteenth century, stood derelict for some time. Bought by the university, some were demolished to make room for the building called New King's, but one block remained. Still called the Old Brewery, it looks much as it always did. The people of Old Aberdeen did not welcome the change and for some time went about saying that they 'could hae dune better wantin' the University than the Brewery'.

Dirty, poorly maintained, cold and draughty, ancient, and generally unsuitable, St Machar's had been kept going by repeated appeals to benefactors and Kirk central funds through the eighteenth century, and later, the Ministry of Works. The strength of its construction, its vast solidity, kept it from falling apart entirely. But as time passed, it began to assume a new kind of importance, as one of the few buildings of the pre-Reformation Scottish church to survive the reformers. As the nineteenth century went on,

the characteristic Victorian interest in Gothic craft and design also renewed interest in it as a building. The 1870s onwards saw major overhauls, which removed the seventeenth-century desks and lofts which had been the subject of so much intense rivalry, equipped the church with gaslight, and gave it new windows. Eventually, new heating was installed and the walls were stripped back to the stone. The work of removing sixty tons of ancient plaster was indescribably dirty, and the loose particles in the air attached themselves to the long rags of cobweb descending from the ceiling, making its dirtiness depressingly clear. There was no money left for erecting scaffolding; in the end, the minister and one of the elders made enormous handles of bamboo cane fastened end to end, and attached them to feather brushes. Risking their necks, they dusted the ceiling as best they could, hanging perilously out of the clerestory: one man cleaned, while the other hung on to him. Their wives were not told until the job had been successfully completed.

Scotland's lost city was well on its way to becoming truly lost, but this is not to say that it did not continue to make its mark in international affairs. One-third of all Aberdeen University graduates joined the military or went into government medical service between 1860 and 1900; in all, about one-quarter worked primarily overseas in the century down to 1950. Additionally, after 1871, members of the university could obtain direct financial assistance from the Wilson Trust Fund for the collection of artefacts from overseas. Partially as a result, King's became a centre of excellence in Egyptology, attracting specialist Egyptologist Nora Macdonald as a conservator and receiving a very important bequest of ancient Egyptian material from James Grant Bey. It is perhaps coincidence that King's alumnus Sir Erasmus Wilson paid an allegedly vast sum to have Cleopatra's Needle, now on the Embankment, shipped from Alexandria to London in 1877.*

Thomas Blake Glover (1838–1911), who was educated at Chanonry House School in Old Aberdeen and lived by the Bridge of Don at 79 Balgownie Road, was one of the most extraordinary characters ever to emerge from the burgh. One of the first Westerners to take advantage of the opening up of Japan to international commerce, he arrived in Nagasaki at the age of twenty-one in 1859 and began to establish himself as an entrepreneur. Japan in the late nineteenth century was undergoing tremendous changes. Although his firm, Glover & Company, became the biggest Western firm in Nagasaki under the last shogun, Glover supported the restoration of Imperial government in 1868. Lord Redesdale, a British diplomat in Japan, noted that Glover was working discreetly on the emperor's behalf, liaising with anti-shogunate domains.

The new Imperial government was aware of his support, and once they had taken power they were not ungrateful. Glover was entrusted with commissioning one of the first warships in the new Imperial Japanese navy, a task which he gave to an Aberdeen shipyard, Alexander Hall & Company. The *Jho Sho Maru*, later *Ryujo Maru*, was fitted out at Blaikie's Quay at a cost of £42,032 and, at her fastest, sailed 264 miles in one day. She was launched on 27 March 1869, and Hall's went on to build two further vessels for Japan.

Glover was also one of the founders of the Japan Brewery Company, makers of Kirin Beer, the oldest beer in Japan and still a leading brand. The image of a kirin (a mythological Japanese

Opposite. The Old Brewery, with Steve Dilworth's bronze sculpture Case *in the foreground.*

* After a dramatic near-sinking in the Bay of Biscay; it did not actually reach England until 1878.

The Old Bridge of Don.

Don, was built by Thomas Blake Glover for his parents in 1864, replacing a humbler house which had been the family home. In 1997, Mitsubishi gave Glover House to the Grampian Japan Trust and it has since been restored to its 1860s appearance with many original details and features. It was opened as a museum celebrating the life and achievements of Thomas Glover, and more broadly, to celebrate and enhance the connections between Scotland and Japan.

Anyone who is minded to visit Glover House will probably be going up King Street. He or she might just notice a granite statue standing by the entrance to St Peter's Catholic School, shortly after the junction of King Street and St Machar Drive, which commemorates one of Aberdeen's most remarkable characters, Charles Gordon – 'Priest' Gordon, as he was generally, and affectionately, known. Born in 1772, he began his studies in the Highland seminary, Scalan, and then went to the Scots College at Douai. He was forced back home by the French Revolution, and for the remainder of his long life, seldom left Aberdeen.

animal) on the label sports an exuberant handlebar moustache which is rumoured to be modelled on Glover's own. He was also involved in the early rise of the Mitsubishi business empire, and played a part in the introduction of railways to Japan. In 1908, he was awarded the Order of the Rising Sun for his services.

Glover took a Japanese wife, Tsuru Awajiya, and it is sometimes alleged that their story was the inspiration for Puccini's *Madama Butterfly*. It is hard to think how, since Tsuru was not a geisha and Glover did not desert her. It is more likely that, since the Glovers were a mixed-race couple, the Nagasaki tourist authorities encouraged this tale for purely commercial reasons. If that was the case, it worked: the Glovers' splendid house in Nagasaki with its panoramic views now attracts two million visitors a year – almost twice as many as Edinburgh Castle.

Glover House, at Balgownie near Bridge of

He was a personality considerably larger than life. Mgr Sandy McWilliam, his successor at St Peter's Church, recorded a story that conveys something of Gordon's humorous, down-to-earth character. His sermons were always interesting, and sometimes unexpected. Preaching on the subject of the Trinity, he declared that the unity of God was a truth every member of the Catholic Church was aware of, and that the youngest child could prove. Unexpectedly, he interrupted himself, and rounded on one of the little boys who was serving at the altar: 'Johnnie, stan' up', he commanded, 'and tell the fouk foo mony gods there are.'

The child, thus unexpectedly addressed, lost his head, and answered 'Three.'

'Sit doon, ye gowk,' said Gordon, greatly put out. 'Ye ken naething aboot it.'

William Clark, an Episcopalian who took an MA at King's and ended his days as professor of theology at Trinity College, Toronto, used often to go to hear Gordon purely for entertainment.

One of the relaxations of the Aberdeen students was to go to the Roman Catholic chapel on Sunday evenings, partly to enjoy the music, partly to listen to the discourses of the Rev. Charles Gordon, the venerable priest in charge of the church. Mr Gordon was a dear old gentleman, Scotch to the backbone; he spoke pretty broad Scotch even in his sermons, was adored by his own people and much respected by the Protestants of Aberdeen. One of the attractions of his chapel was his practice of preaching strongly Roman and anti-Protestant sermons on Sunday evenings. Martin Luther and John Knox were held up to universal execration in the most delightful broad Scotch and with a vehemence that might have satisfied the Grand Inquisitor. Occasionally these attacks produced bursts of merriment from his Protestant hearers and if these became audible – which they sometimes did – the culprit was ejected by the sexton. This was no unusual occurrence since the laughter was sometimes unavoidable and the sexton was always on the watch.

Thomas Blake Glover (second from right).

Priest Gordon had a very Scottish dry humour. When he was challenged by a Protestant on the Catholic doctrine of Purgatory, his response was 'Weel. A' I hiv tae say, Doctor, is that we can gang farrer and fare waur!' It is something of the measure of the man that his biography was written not by a fellow Catholic, but by a Congregationalist, a minister from one of the most radical of Protestant dissenting traditions who, nonetheless, saw in him one of God's great men. Energetic, practical and a man of the widest human charity, Gordon founded the first St Peter's School in 1833. At his funeral in 1855, so many townsmen and women joined the procession that it was still leaving the New Town's Castlegate when the head of the cortège reached the Old Town's Snow Kirk. Alexander Brodie, a local sculptor, was given a commission for a commemorative statue of Gordon, which since 1859 has accompanied the school through its several migrations.

CHAPTER THREE

Treasures of Old Aberdeen

The collections of an ancient university inevitably become a microcosm of the known world; a representation of the development of knowledge of the world, and all that it contains. Aberdeen University's holdings can realistically be described as one of the oldest public collections in the English-speaking world, especially when one bears in mind that, until the later eighteenth century, there was no hard and fast distinction between the different types of collection that would now be divided into library and museum. Manuscripts, paintings, prints, scientific instruments, botanical specimens and curiosities coexist in a continuum, public and semi-public, in and out of doors. They combine to create a cornerstone of a university and a

Opposite. St Machar's Cathedral from the east.

Engraving by F.C. Lewis, from a painting by Alexander Nasmyth, 1808.

Part of an engraved panorama by Clérisseau from Robert Adam's The Ruins of the Palace of Diocletian at Spalatro.

Opposite top. A plate from the Aberdeen Bestiary, *illustrating the legend that a tiger will try to nurse a mirrored ball, thinking it is her cub.*

Opposite bottom left. The ibex, meanwhile, could fall from a great height and be saved by his horns.

Opposite bottom right. The hyena: hermaphrodite and tomb-dweller.

burgh that have never lost sight of the Renaissance vision and energy which brought them into being. As such, they provide a major resource for the use of not only the university, but also of the people of the region, of Scotland, and of the international scholarly community.

Books and Manuscripts

The university's Special Collections include more than a quarter of a million early printed books and manuscripts, many of which are of great beauty, value, and historical importance. Enquirers outwith the university can use the library and its collections. Recently, two of its most remarkable manuscripts, the *Bestiary* (see box, p.108) and the Burnet Psalter, have been fully digitised, and are now readily accessible via the internet.

The King's College copy of the *Polychronicon*, or *Universal History*, written by John Higden (d. 1364) a monk of St Werberg, Chester,

is particularly handsome. This was the most complete one-volume history book of the fourteenth century, which, as its author claimed, went 'from the beginning of the world to the death of King Edward III in seven books'. A medieval bestseller, it was translated into English from the original Latin by John of Trevisa in 1387, at the behest of Thomas, Lord Berkeley. The English *Polychronicon* appealed greatly to kings and nobles as soon as it was translated, and thus it is not surprising that among more than a hundred surviving manuscripts there are some very beautiful copies with illuminated initials and decorated pages, aimed at, or commissioned for, members of the aristocracy. Aberdeen's copy is one such. It has illuminated borders to the seven books and the table of contents, and initials for the chapters. Two illustrations are particularly attractive. The best is of Higden himself, in his Benedictine robes, writing on a desk fixed across the arms of his chair, as in many a modern lecture theatre. The other is of a curious, double-decker Noah's Ark. The

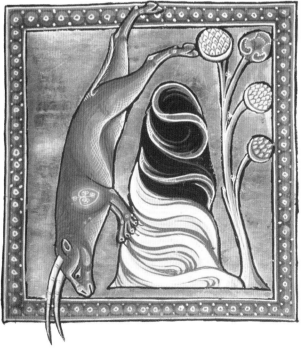

The *Bestiary*

The bear sculpts her cub from formless matter with her tongue.

One of the earliest treasures of the university's collection, conserved at King's College, is a sumptuous manuscript, written and illuminated in England around the year 1200, which attempts to encompass the world within its pages. It is known as the *Aberdeen Bestiary*, but goes well beyond the descriptions of animals implied by this title, to attempt an account of all God's works in nature. This 'book of the visible world' includes animals and birds, fishes, plants, monsters and imaginary beings. The cat and the dog share creation with the phoenix and the unicorn, and with the mysterious royal bird called Caladrius which can take upon itself the sickness of a king and carry that disease away to the sun.

The text is fantastical and delightful: the tiger sees herself in a glass sphere and thinks that her own reflection is her cub; the fox rolls in red earth and pretends to be dead to lure birds within his reach; the hedgehog spears fallen grapes on her spines to carry them back to her babies.

The manuscript is profusely illustrated. The pictures of the creatures emerge from burnished metal-leaf backgrounds, a golden world hinting at the purposes and designs of its Creator. There is an extraordinary illumination of the creation of the beasts at the beginning of the manuscript, and there are spectacular symbolic pages for the dove and for the cedar. Throughout, the sense of design is unfaltering, so that even humble insects are still depicted in boldly designed patterns in front of their burnished and shining grounds.

The painting is immensely skilled, capable of such sophisticated effects as the egg-white varnish laid over the white plumage of the swan to make it shimmer on the page, or the beautifully poised illustration of the phoenix between two subtly swaying trees, under the heat of a fierce sun.

The interest of the *Aberdeen Bestiary* is deepened by the inclusion in its margins of some working sketches, and the survival in the manuscript of other indications of the techniques by which it was made: tracings and pouncings of outlines, and the little marginal letters with which the scribe has cued the illuminator to place the painted and gilded initials.

This is one of the finest manuscripts of its type to survive, and its outstanding quality suggests that it may have been made for a royal patron, possibly Geoffrey Plantagenet, illegitimate son of King Henry II. The most likely place of origin for it is in a scriptorium in the north of England, and current scholarship suggests that it was illuminated in Bridlington in Yorkshire. It corresponds exactly in text and arrangement of illustrations to the *Ashmolean Bestiary* in the Bodleian Library in Oxford. The two manuscripts are sisters, of the same family, but with very different illustrations. The *Oxford Bestiary* is in general static and Gothic in the design of its pictures where the *Aberdeen Bestiary* is Romanesque, its illustrator more interested in movement than repose.

The manuscript used to reside in the old Royal Library at Westminster Palace. It still bears its Westminster shelf mark of no. 158 and is recognisable in the shelf list made in 1542. In the early seventeenth century it appears to have been presented to Thomas Reid, regent of Marischal College and Latin secretary to James VI. It is possible that it came to him on his retirement from royal service, either as a gift or in settlement of salary still due to him. It came to Aberdeen as part of Reid's 1624 gift of over a thousand books and manuscripts.

The *Bestiary* has now been digitised in full and can be accessed online, with translations and explanations of the text.

The fox feigns death by rolling in red earth and holding his breath.

manuscript was previously owned by John, Lord Hay of Yester, a Scottish nobleman, whose interest in fine books is also evidenced by two manuscripts bearing his signature, now in the Pepysian Library at Magdalene College, Cambridge.

The university also holds a priceless illuminated codex of the Hebrew Bible (see box, p.112), dating to the winter of 1493–94, bequeathed by Professor Thomas Reid in the 1620s. The codex contains the complete text, written in double column, together with the commentary known as the *massorah magna*, and various prayers and blessings written in the margins in a wonderfully inventive ornamented *tour de force* of patterned calligraphy.

Among the many interesting early printed books at King's is Thomas Harriot's *A Wonderful and Faithful Narration of the Goods and Religion of the Inhabitants of Virginia* (Frankfurt am Main, 1590), illustrated by Theodore de Bry. One fascinating feature of this volume is the presence in it, alongside maps of the coastline and the interior, of sketches of fishing methods and other native crafts such as how to build a canoe, and of villages and people of various ranks and types. It also features an antiquarian appendix on the primitive inhabitants of Britain that compares their way of life, clothes, and warfare with those of contemporary Native Americans.

A whole collection of important books and manuscripts came into the college's possession as the gift of the bibliophile and bookseller James Fraser. Born in Inverness-shire and educated at King's, Fraser appears to have acted as private librarian to Charles II and James II at Whitehall. There is no doubt that Fraser moved in the most educated and scientific circles in Britain, buying

Above. The murder of St Thomas of Canterbury, from The Golden Legend, *printed by Caxton, with sixteenth-century deletions ordered by Henry VIII.*

Left. From Zakariya Ibn Muhammed Al-Qazwini's The Wonders of Creation, *an Arabic manuscript of* c.1700.

ラツトセイ
脳明瞭

and selling books for many of the most distinguished scholars of his day. He also left 1,051 valuable books to King's library, as well as the then substantial sum of £1,600 for a new library building.

The university's Special Collections also contain a variety of fascinating travellers' accounts. Between 1666 and 1670, a different James Fraser (1634–1709), Episcopalian minister of Kirkhill near Inverness, kept diaries in his twenties of his extensive tour of Britain and Western Europe, which he called *Triennial Travels*. His three manuscript volumes are preserved as Aberdeen University manuscript number 2,538 and have yet to be transcribed or studied at length. Almost unknown and unpublished, Fraser's journal is nevertheless one of the most remarkable and substantial texts from early-modern Britain. He was a superb recorder of the minutiae of daily life, particularly in the London of 1657 – the statue of King Charles I at the Royal Exchange broken to pieces and an inscription, 'Exit Tyrannus', set up in its place. A staunch royalist, like most King's alumni, he comments, 'O with what a bleeding heart and blubering eyes did I read it.' He saw a prominent Quaker placed in the pillory for alleged blasphemy, and viewed with shame the captured banners of Scottish royalist regiments hanging in Westminster Hall: 'it truly galled my spirit and dashed my very soule to behold them.' He jotted down the opening lines of a new libel of Cromwell which some brave royalist had nailed to Whitehall Gate: 'If any strangers do but know what Cromwell doth here, he's profitable to the state for he can brewe good beere.' As well as extensive entries made during his continental travels, on his return to Britain at the time of the Restoration, Fraser had some interesting things to say about King's College itself.

Dr Robert Wilson (1787–1871), another Aberdeen alumnus, travelled still further afield. 'After a long and weary journey which embraced almost every country which has emblazoned the page of sacred or profane history, from Carthage to the Indus', he arrived in India towards the end of a staggering odyssey across the Middle East. A landowner's son from Banffshire, educated at Marischal College, Wilson began his travelling life as surgeon to the Honourable East India Company. He made his last voyage with them in 1809, and in 1816 took advantage of the defeat of the Napoleonic forces in Europe and embarked on a delayed Grand Tour in the manner of the eighteenth century. Then, in 1820, he ventured eastwards partly to see the Egyptian and Middle Eastern antiquities newly described by the scholars who had accompanied Napoleon's Egyptian campaigns.

Wilson's journals, all spaciously laid out on the pages of ample vellum-bound folios with handsome drawings and watercolours tipped in as illustration, include details of his journey up the Nile as far as Abu Simbel, which had been discovered only in 1813 by the explorer J.L. Burckhardt. He was one of the first European travellers to follow in Burckhardt's footsteps. Another particularly important adventure was his expedition to view the ruins of Persepolis, the capital of Persia at the time of Alexander the Great, near the modern city of Shiraz in Iran. This was written up in a detailed account with many documentary drawings of sculptures and antiquities. Given the history of Iran in more recent years, some of these may well be the only records of artefacts which have since been lost or destroyed. The texts vividly illustrate the difficulties of Asian exploration in the early

Opposite top. From New Year's Ceremonies of the Ezo People at Matsumae Castle, *a Japanese scroll painting painted between 1807 and 1856.*

Opposite bottom. The Ainu people of the islands of Honshu and Hokkaido, who were included in the term 'Ezo', hand-reared bears, which they treated as gods. Only one other such scroll is known to survive in a British collection.

The Hebrew Bible

Old Aberdeen's codex of the Hebrew Bible was written in exile by a Sephardic scribe, Isaac ben David Balsani, whose name indicates that his family originated in Valencia in Spain. He was working for a patron from one of the oldest and most honoured Jewish families of Spain, Joseph Albelia, who had also been recently expelled from his native land by the edict of the king issued in 1492.

The greater part of the work was almost certainly undertaken at Naples in the brief period of peace enjoyed by the Jewish community there before the violent disruptions caused by Charles VIII of France's invasion in February 1495. The Aberdeen codex offers a brief glimpse of the kind of work which would have been created for enlightened Jewish patrons of the high Renaissance, had circumstances offered more interludes of peace to the Sephardic communities of southern Europe. The colophon which the scribe added to his work certainly expresses hopes for the future: 'may the Almighty make him worthy to study it, he and his sons and his sons' sons.' But, even before the last small corrections were made to this glorious manuscript, it was abandoned, presumably as a result of the arrival of the French army. Thus the tables of variant reading which precede the text are lacking the pointing-marks which would render them complete.

The fine illuminations framing these columns of variants are the work of professional illuminators and show a cosmopolitan range of artistic influences. There are two complementary styles: one looks to medieval painting as exemplified in the stately dance of heraldic animals, including two rampant lions of Judah, which preface the Book of Isaiah. This painter probably also undertook the borders of densely woven scrolls of foliage, with heraldry and animals decoratively placed amongst the leaves that ornament some of these preliminary pages of variants. This work is rich and intricate, following a tradition of ornamenting manuscript margins with patterns of stylised foliage, heightened by points of gold and brighter colour.

The second style of illumination looks to the Renaissance rediscoveries of the architecture and artefacts of classical antiquity, as shown by the highly sophisticated architectural fantasies that frame other pages of the tables of variants; the sacred text itself is decorated only with calligraphy. These colonnades, coloured in delicate reds and purples, are represented illusionistically in perspective. Animals and birds, rendered in three dimensions, inhabit their ledges and cornices. On one leaf, there is a delicate landscape receding between the first and second columns on the left, a sun emerging from cloud shooting thin lines of gold leaf across an azure sky. Other leaves are ornamented by reconstructions of the tall candelabra of antiquity.

Sometimes the history implied by a manuscript – and manuscripts of this quality inevitably tell their own story – can be almost as moving as the quality of the work itself. The Aberdeen codex of the Hebrew Bible is not only an object of great beauty and rarity, it is also an important object of memory within the history of Europe in all its compexity. This manuscript was particularly admired by the great Dr Samuel Johnson when he visited Aberdeen in August 1773.

From the Aberdeen codex of the Hebrew Bible, 1493–94.

nineteenth century. In his journey through the Ottoman territories of Palestine and Syria, Wilson had to assume Arab dress and pretend to be the servant of Yusuf, his guide. Despite these precautions, in the course of his travels through what were once the ancient empires of Assyria and Babylonia, he was briefly held prisoner by the Kurds.

The Indian volume of the travels is perhaps the most eloquent: Wilson was very much at his ease in pre-mutiny India, adopting native dress, and using the extensive network of contacts and friends which he had acquired through his years working for the East India Company. The highlight of this journey was his visit to Agra, where he bought jewel-coloured and gilded gouache paintings of the Red Fort for his journal. He greatly appreciated 'the unearthly beauty of the Tauge Mahal', as he calls it, particularly when seen from amidst the cypresses and 'select shrubberies' of the formal gardens. His views were expansive, his interests cultivated, and his bravery unquestionable. The whole assembly of Wilson's manuscripts (of which there are thirty in Old Aberdeen) offers considerable scope for research and study, not only in the context of the history of travel, but also because they include pioneering works of archaeology.

William MacBean, who was born in Nairn, Aberdeenshire, in 1856, became a successful businessman in New York. A member (and historian) of the New York St Andrew's Society, MacBean was an enthusiast for that most Aberdonian of causes, Jacobitism. Over his lifetime he assembled a magnificent collection of Jacobite material, which he donated to Aberdeen University in 1918. The MacBean Stuart and Jacobite Collection is a resource of international importance, the finest collection of its kind outside the British Library, containing numerous items held in no other collection in the UK. Some 3,500 books and 1,000 pamphlets, as well as numerous engravings, cover many aspects of the histories of the Stuart royal family and the Jacobite risings which attempted to restore them to the throne. From the year 1688 the three kingdoms of Scotland, Ireland and England had, in effect, two monarchs, two courts, two aristocracies, and twin and conflicting demands on the loyalty of their citizens. For the Jacobite heartlands in northern Scotland, particularly the traditionally conservative Episcopalian and Catholic territories of Aberdeenshire and Banffshire, the battle of Culloden ended a way of life based on traditional loyalties and customs, and in so doing brought in, often forcibly, the modernisation of rural life and society. It would be possible to say that there were two *realities* fighting for the citizens' loyalty and belief. So absolutely did either side refuse to acknowledge the status of the opposition, to the loyal Whig the exiled James was 'the Old Pretender', and to the court in exile Queen Anne was merely 'the Princess of Denmark'. The MacBean collection documents the wars of loyalty fought out in pamphlet form during these troubled years.

John Gould's superb *Introduction to the Trochilidae, or Humming Birds* appeared as a serial from 1845–61 and is representative of Old Aberdeen's particularly fine collection of colour-plate books from the eighteenth and nineteenth centuries. As illustration techniques had developed from the Renaissance onwards, beginning with the engravings of the first collections of natural and artificial curiosities, more and more of the natural world was brought into the lithographed museum of the colour-plate

Blake illustrations from Thornton's Pastorals of Virgil *(1821).*

To face page 18.

ILLUSTRATIONS OF IMITATION OF ECLOGUE I.

THENOT. To illustrate lines 1, 2.

3, 4, 5, 6.

7, 8, 9.

10.

books. An ornithologist and publisher, Gould (1804–81) was responsible for a series of large-folio illustrated books, published in monthly parts, which took as their subject the natural history of the whole world. A Victorian self-made man, Gould had begun his career as a taxidermist, but made his mark with the volume on birds which he contributed to Charles Darwin's *Voyage of the Beagle*. The artists for his lithographed volumes of ornithology included his wife Elizabeth Coxen Gould (1804–41) and Edward Lear (1812–88), who was a professional painter though he is now more famous for his nonsense verse. The global scope of Gould's enterprise was confirmed by his publication, after extensive travels, of *Birds of Australia* in 1840–48, and his participation in the Great Exhibition of 1851, during which his building in the London Zoological Gardens provided an environment for his live hummingbirds. By this time he had already embarked on the vast *Birds of Asia* which appeared from 1850–83.

The finest of all his illustrated books is his volume of hummingbirds, lithographed and hand-coloured. In his desire to represent faithfully the darting iridescence of the birds, Gould used techniques familiar from the illuminated manuscripts of the middle ages and Renaissance. To represent the effects of light and movement on the feather of this 'Gorgeted Sun Angel' hummingbird, Gould used varnish and metal leaf applied over the hand-coloured lithograph – similar special effects are used in the *Aberdeen Bestiary*.

Smaller in scale, but no less important, the seventeen wood engravings which William Blake contributed to the 1821 edition of *The Pastorals of Virgil, with a course of English reading, adapted for schools* are among his most influential works, and also among his last. The text was the work of Robert Thornton, physician, botanist, and the compiler of the finest illustrated botanical book of the eighteenth century, *The Temple of Flora*. Blake was introduced to him by the artist John Linnel, and contracted to provide illustrations to the third edition of his Virgil. This publication was intended as a progressive schoolbook, designed to engage the pupils' interest, and to help them to read Virgil's universally admired *Eclogues* or pastoral poems. To this end, not only are Virgil's texts interspersed with poems in English, they are also presented in the form of 'imitations', that is, translations which transform the setting of the poems from ancient Italy to modern England. To aid the young reader, each important narrative element or striking image in these imitations is illustrated by a small woodblock, designed to fix the text in the visual as well as verbal memory. The extraordinary response which this seemingly mundane publication drew from the ageing Blake changed the course of British art.

Pictures, Maps and Sculpture

It could be argued that the first curatorial decision taken by King's College was the preservation, at the Reformation, of an oil-on-panel portrait of Bishop Elphinstone. Thought to have been painted from life, probably by a Flemish artist, it dates to approximately 1505. Exceptionally for Scotland, even though it presumably once formed part of the altarpiece of the chapel, it was not destroyed as a 'rag of popery', but preserved out of respect for the college's founder.

A bust of Malcolm Hay of Seaton in the office of Father James Claffey.

As we have seen, the first principal of King's, historian Hector Boece, had been educated at the Sorbonne and remained in touch with the exploratory continental humanist movement. The reclamation of the classical past went hand in hand with other ways of pushing back the frontiers of the known. Geography, in particular, became a focus of intellectual energy from the late fifteenth century, as the world expanded to include reports of the fabulous territories across the Atlantic, as well as the northern ice-fields and the empires of Asia. The dream of a connected world seemed to be in the process of realisation. It is for this reason that King's holds such an excellent collection of early atlases, including Boece's own copy of the Greek scholar Ptolemy's atlas (1482), which lacks America. But Ptolemy was periodically brought up to date: in the edition of 1513, also held in Old Aberdeen, the south-east coast of America begins to emerge from the mist of conjecture. The Gulf of Mexico, Florida, Cuba and the Caribbean are, literally, on the map, whereas to the north and south the firm lines of the coast gradually dissolve into

uncertainty. By the time of the great Mercator atlas of a century later, America had been superbly mapped, and was recognisable in outline, even though much of the western coast and interior still remained *terra incognita* until the Lewis and Clark expedition of 1804–06.

A different kind of geographic text, *Civitates Orbis Terrarum*, edited by Georg Braun (1541–1622), a clergyman of Cologne, depicts the cities of the world. It was published in a series which began in 1572, and emerged from the circle of the great geographer Abraham Ortelius (1527–98) as a deliberate counterpart to Ortelius's atlas, the *Theatrum Orbis Terrarum*. The engraver Franz Hogenberg (1535–90), a Bavarian living in the Spanish Netherlands, worked on both projects. These men were equally the products of that group of northern European scholars, travellers, artists and printers who were the first to try to understand the whole of the geography of the earth. Although they achieved an exponential advance in the mapping of Europe and the New World, the edges of their vision still faded, at the extremes of north and south, into uncertain territories, regions peopled by the monsters and wonders of the medieval imagination.

The *Civitates* drew on the skills of more than a hundred different artists and geographers, the most eminent of whom was the scholar and painter Joris Hoefnagel (1542–1600), who contributed the drawings of Spanish and Italian cities which formed the basis of Hogenberg's engravings. Through Hoefnagel, this publication – in itself an epitome of the world – is linked to the bizarre museum of the wonders of the world that was formed in Prague by the Emperor Rudolph II, at whose court Hoefnagel worked in the 1590s.

These volumes of fine engravings document a Europe grown fragile from wars of religion, a Europe divided against itself and menaced from the east by the Ottoman Empire. To an extent, the views of cities are offered as a means of travelling in the imagination through regions where physical travel had grown problematic and dangerous. Braun wrote that he had included the figures in the typical clothes of each city in the foreground, not only for their intrinsic interest, but also as a device to prevent his book from being used for military intelligence by the Turks, who, it was thought, would be repelled by the (to them, illicit) representations of the human figure. To the modern reader, *Civitates Orbis Terrarum* offers the illusion of being able to travel in time and to see cities – familiar and unfamiliar – as once they were, before the devastations of the wars of the churches and empires.

The university also has a number of interesting pictures, some commissioned by the college, some collected by it. Elphinstone is not the only historical figure associated with King's to have a surviving portrait there. Another is John Lesley: bishop of Ross, historian, Catholic, Old Aberdeen professor of canon law, and defender of Mary, Queen of Scots. For all that he was a highly controversial figure, King's must have taken steps to acquire his portrait since it is probably French and dates from the last stage of Lesley's career when he was bishop of Coutances in Normandy.

George Jamesone, son of the Aberdeen mason-architect who restored the Brig o' Balgownie, was one of the most successful and talented British-born professional painters of the seventeenth century. A variety of paintings attributed to him are held in the King's collection, including a portrait of his close friend,

Opposite. Two plates from Civitates Orbis Terrarum.

the Latin poet Arthur Johnston, as well as likenesses of the Scougalls and of many other figures of significance in the Aberdeen Renaissance. Many of these show real skill, quality and gravitas. Unfortunately, Jamesone either experimented with paint, or had difficulty getting good-quality colours. Some of the pigments he used were fugitive, so few of his surviving works have escaped the efforts of restorers of varying skill. The real quality of *Arthur Johnston*, in exceptionally good and possibly original condition, makes this a matter for serious regret. Another of Jamesone's King's pictures which survives in good condition is a portrait of James Sandilands, professor of civil law, with its sunflower impresa and motto *splendente vivo secedente pereo*: 'I live by reflecting [the sun]; I perish by turning away from it'. Also by Jamesone, but seriously affected by the deterioration of his pigments, are the ten survivors of the original twelve Aberdeen Sibyls (see box, p.120), which were commissioned for the Common Hall of King's in the 1640s to replace the portraits of the disgraced Aberdeen Doctors who had opposed the National Covenant.

Among the most historically interesting pictures in the collection are the so-called Black Paintings, which have been cleaned, and are no longer as murky as they used to be. They are a series of mid-seventeenth century panels on canvas of Old Testament scenes with borders feigning tapestry, which are on display in Elphinstone Hall. These are rare survivors of ephemeral early-modern pictures made for a special occasion – in this case, the occasion was the hastily constructed presence chamber of Charles II, made when he returned to Scotland to make his first, abortive, attempt to regain his thrones in 1650. Worldwide, there are only two

or three comparable sets: canvases survive from festivals in Antwerp and Florence, and there is a 1621 set of panels from the last ducal wedding in Urbino. But in a British context, this survival is unique, and a vivid illustration of how the fine arts could be used to create a public discourse regarding government. In this case, they carried a blunt message which menaced and humiliated the boy-king enthroned amongst the Presbyterian ministers' reproaches and warnings.

The Black Paintings were probably produced to be hung in Gowrie House, which served briefly as a royal residence. The south wall of the hall there had five windows, and reading from the left-hand side, the five paintings – *Jephthah*, *David and Goliath*, *David and Abigail*, *The Judgment of Solomon*, and *Solomon and Sheba* – would have been hung in order around the room. There are five spaces between the windows, suggesting that the paintings occupied these five positions. But wherever they hung, the paintings appear to have been designed to function in a manner akin to emblems, instructing the viewer in moral and ethical matters.

The conservatism of King's, and its resistance to the radical reforms of the seventeenth century, combined to give it an attitude to collecting and preserving visual art which was not at all characteristic of Scotland in the early-modern era. One area, perhaps the only area, to remain wholly 'safe' in this respect was heraldry. Predating the Reformation by something over 300 years, heraldry and its practitioners remained resolutely secular. By the sixteenth century, Lutherans, Calvinists, Jews, Catholics, and even some Native American leaders were patronising the herald painters and participating on equal terms in this transnational, non-confessional symbolic system. It is probably no coincidence

Opposite. Four of the 'Black Paintings', c.1651

The Sibyls

Among the treasures and curiosities of Old Aberdeen are a set of ten paintings, survivors of a set of twelve, of the Sibyls: legendary women of the ancient world who were believed in Christian tradition to have experienced prophetic visions of aspects of the life of Christ. This sequence of paintings was commissioned by William Guild (principal of King's, 1640–51) and was placed in the old Common Hall of the college, where they remained for many years. Though very much a Protestant who supervised the removal of overtly Catholic images and symbols from St Machar's Cathedral, Principal Guild was a moderate one, who did this only after consultation and consideration.

The paintings of the Sibyls represent one of the very first commissions of art for public display in Scotland, and in the turbulent decade of their creation represented an ingenious, even brilliant, choice of subject unlikely to give offence to any shade of religious opinion. The kind of visual art most acceptable to rigid Calvinists was the representation of scriptural history or, even less controversially, of exemplary or heroic figures. The Sibyls accord with this as prophets, granted the exceptional privilege of access to religious truth. Their likenesses are not liable even to elicit the kind of excessive veneration which Calvinists feared might be accorded to representations of figures from the Bible. To the moderate Protestants who would later form the Episcopalian community with its more relaxed, Lutheran attitude to the visual arts, the Sibyls would be of especial interest as figures representing the revelation of Christianity to the Gentiles, their status sanctioned in the writings of St Augustine, one of the revered Fathers of the Western Church. For Old Aberdeen's community of élite Catholics, the representation of the Sibyls alongside the prophets of the Old Testament was sanctioned by centuries of tradition.

It is widely believed that the paintings were undertaken in the studio of the celebrated George Jamesone, who was born in Aberdeen and was related to Principal Guild. Although the Sibyls bear some resemblance to portraits painted by Jamesone at the height of his career, they are clearly derived from a series of engravings by Crispin van de Passe the

Sibyl Cumea.

Elder (1567–1637), *XII Sibyllarum Icones Elegantissimi*, published in 1601. Scans of the original paint layer undertaken by art historian Dr Mary Pryor revealed the ghosts of paintings of a quality consistent with Jamesone's surviving work. However, a century of exposure to the smoke from fire and candles in the Common Hall had caused Jamesone's images to fade dramatically by the mid-eighteenth century. (Indeed, the two missing Sibyls may have simply decayed beyond repair at that time.) Clearly the Sibyls were considered in some sense part of the identity and tradition of the university because the civil law professor of the day paid for restoration work on them which amounts, in fact, to an almost complete overpainting. This repainting was undertaken in 1761 by a descendant of Jamesone's, the outlaw portraitist Cosmo Alexander (1724–72), a Catholic whose career encompassed service in the Jacobite armies and exile in Rome as well as periods of prosperity in London and America. Alexander signed and dated his work on the book held by the Egyptian Sibyl. It is to his intervention that we can attribute the elegance and charm of the figures in their present state, with their slender hands and elegantly painted jewels. It is also possible that he subtly emphasised some of the symbolic objects carried by the Sibyls – for instance, Europa's sceptre and the rose carried by Cumea – to accord with the essentially conservative religious and political traditions of Old Aberdeen. He would almost certainly have had access to de Passe's prints for reference, but could have drawn also on personal knowledge of Baroque Sibyl-cycles in Italy and the Low Countries.

Some of the symbols carried by this Old Aberdeen sequence of Sibyls, like the crown of thorns held by the Samian Sibyl, refer to events in the life of Christ. Others, including the palm branches carried by the Phrygian and Libyan Sibyls and the Erythrean Sibyl's lamb, are symbols of marytrdom. But some, like the sceptre, the rose or the sword, are more widely allusive, bearing as much reference to temporal royal governance as to the divine kingship of Christ.

For all these reasons, these paintings are rightly amongst the treasures of King's College, whose conservatism, tolerance and loyalty are represented on their canvases.

Sibyl Erythrea.

that King's College, one of early-modern Britain's most eirenic institutions, would fly its heraldic achievements like a flag. High on the walls of the inner quad at King's one can see a dozen heraldic tablets, mostly seventeenth century, carved in high relief, painted and gilded. The arms displayed include those of King James IV, Hector Boece, the royal librarian James Fraser, and bishops Elphinstone, Dunbar, and Stewart.

On the chapel's west front, five feet high, three feet wide, and twenty feet in the air, one finds the oldest extant use of two unicorns as supporters for the arms of Scotland. Dating to 1504, this sculpture is one year older than a similar one on the westernmost buttress of Melrose Abbey. That this was not known until 1888 typifies the way in which Scottish heraldic art can be taken for granted – an extreme case being the non-discovery of the Bishop Elphinstone armorial misericord, which went undescribed, if not necessarily unseen, until 2006. A treasure within a treasure, the misericord is carved in the underside of a child's seat less than fourteen inches square in the chapel's original, *c.*1506–09, oak choir stalls, themselves a unique survival. Of more than 8,000 pre-Reformation misericords known to exist in Europe, fewer than 200 feature heraldry, and of these, just eighteen – including Elphinstone's – bear the arms of bishops, archbishops, or episcopal sees. The choir stalls' eight other surviving misericords include the sacred monogram 'IHS', a crowned saltire long misidentified as a chevron, and a very early use of thistles as a symbol of the nation.

Nor does Old Aberdeen's heraldry pertain only to the university. The burgh cross and St Machar's magnificent armorial ceiling, both dating to the reign of James V, have already been described (Chapter Two, above). The arms of the burgh itself appear three times on King's Chapel's lead-clad Caroline spire, but also above the door of the Town House on a plaque which predates the construction of the building itself by more than fifty years. The gates of Powis Gate bear the arms of the Leslies of Powis, as does at least one house in the High Street, while on a relatively modest house in Balgownie one may see personal arms dating from 1655.

Perhaps because it short-circuited Calvinist iconophobia, early-modern heraldic art in Aberdeenshire and the North-east generally achieved a form which elsewhere in Europe might have been called excessive. On nearby castles – themselves thicker on the ground in Aberdeenshire than anywhere else in Scotland, if not the British Isles – not merely the male owner's arms would be carved, but those of his wife, his feudal superiors, perhaps those of *their* wives, and even the arms of the builder. Huntly Castle represents an extreme case, with a veritable stack of heraldic tablets reaching to nearly four times the height of the front door, but Tolquhon Castle and others give Huntly a run for its money. One is tempted to suppose that the (oddly expensive) choice of soft imported sandstone for King's was part of a far-sighted plan that similar stacks of heraldic carving would one day adorn the chapel's buttresses.

In the event, the university's passion for all

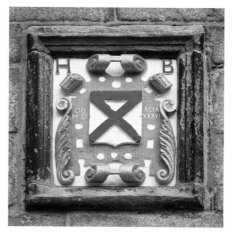

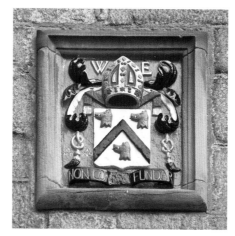

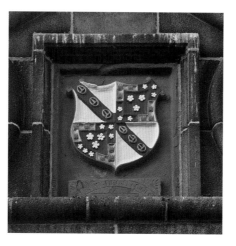

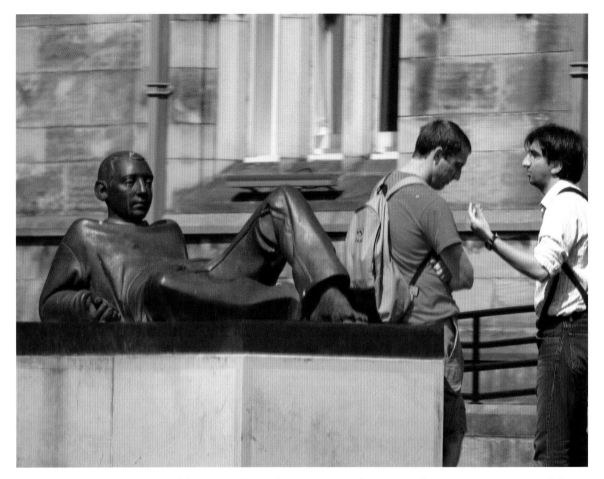

Kenny Hunter's Youth with Split Apple – *better known to the students as 'Igor'.*

things heraldic would spread horizontally rather than vertically. A dozen more coats of arms may be seen from Elphinstone Lawn. Though almost all of these date to after 1900, they include the only Scottish example of the full heraldic achievement James IV's consort, Margaret Tudor – source of the Stuarts' claim to the throne of England, realised in 1603. Another seven coats appear over the entrance to Marischal College. This is to say nothing of the old town's cast-metal armorial bollards, heraldry on cars and vans, or the heraldic neckties of scores of student clubs, teams and societies.

The university's art-collecting efforts have persisted into modern times, augmented by a number of generous gifts. Elphinstone's memorial (see box, p.126) is one of the university's more spectacular commissions of the last hundred years, but the tradition continues. Relatively recent acquisitions include works by Douglas Strachan, Elizabeth Blackadder, Sir Terry Frost, Robin Philipson, Walter Sickert, Callum Innes, Ian Hamilton Finlay, and Barbara Rae. A considerable variety of sculpture can be found on public display around the campus. One notable highlight, located outside New King's, is Kenny Hunter's *Youth with Split Apple* – better known to the students as 'Igor'.

Opposite. Arms, clockwise from top left: the burgh of Old Aberdeen, Hector Boece, unidentified, Patrick Forbes, William Stewart, Leslie of Powis, King James IV, and Gavin Dunbar, with William Elphinstone in the centre.

The Elphinstone Memorial

This remarkable structure is a conspicuous, and curious, part of the landscape of the High Street, sited as it is in the middle of the lawn outside the chapel, at some distance from the west door. It was originally intended as a re-creation of Elphinstone's tomb, which was erected by his successor Bishop Dunbar, and carefully described in the college inventory of 1542 as

> his effigy in bishop's vestments, with two angels carrying two candlesticks at the head and two beadsmen carrying the epitaph graven in brass at the feet; below, on the south side are the three theological Virtues and Contemplation; on the north side are the four cardinal Virtues distinguished by their emblems; on the east and west sides the arms of the Founder carried by angels.

James Gordon's description of Aberdeen offers a slightly different vision of the monument. In his description, a black touchstone slab covered the grave – as it still does – but a second, identical stone was upheld by thirteen bronze statues. According to Gordon, the effigy of the bishop lay on the lower stone as if in a four-poster bed. But Gordon was writing from at least twenty years' distance; 'all these,' he says, were 'robbed and sold long ago'. It would have been more usual to have a bishop's effigy lying on the upper slab. Many contemporary monuments filled the space beneath with a second effigy representing the decaying corpse on the lower level, a fashion that greatly added to the expense of construction and which

seems not to have been attempted in this case.

The monument on King's lawn originated with Principal William Geddes's restoration of the chapel in the early years of the twentieth century. With the 400th anniversary of Elphinstone's death coming up, various schemes were mooted for some kind of memorial. In 1909, the college finally settled on the idea of recreating Dunbar's tomb, based on the 1542 account. They did not want a pastiche of a late-medieval monument, but something in a modern idiom using the same elements that were mentioned as part of the original design. The committee found itself increasingly drawn to one particular artist, Henry Wilson (1864–1934), one of the central figures of the Arts and Crafts Movement, whose approach seemed to them both sympathetic and original.

Henry Wilson was an artist whose originality bordered on the maverick. He was trained, and occasionally practised, as an architect, but as time went on he was more and more attracted to creating fittings rather than buildings: to metalwork, sculpture, and even jewellery. His appearance, 'like a seedy bank clerk', gave no hint of his passionate, impractical, and idealistic nature.

The committee stipulated that the monument should be completed by 31 May 1913, suggesting that they hoped to unveil it at Elphinstone's 400th anniversary celebrations (in October 1914), cannily allowing some slack for assembly, artistic temperament and last-minute problems. But they did not have the measure of their man. Wilson procrastinated. The deadline passed and the First World War broke out, providing one reason for delay. Wilson's serious illness in 1915 gave another.

When he recovered, he put much of his energy into the Art Workers' Guild; he also mounted the 1916 Arts and Crafts exhibition at the Royal Academy. The war came to an end and there was still no monument. Representations from Aberdeen were met by requests for more money, and more time.

Wilson's view, quite clearly, was that nothing whatever should interfere with his creative process. The monument would take whatever time it needed to come to birth, and contracts had nothing to do with it. It was the masterpiece that mattered. There was very little that Aberdeen could do. Doubtless there was one set of voices arguing that they should drop the whole thing and stop throwing good money after bad, and another that they should sue the artist for breach of contract. A peace party, led by the professor of Greek, argued for patience – and found themselves forced to do so again and again and again.

The thirteen figures of the Virtues and Vices which support the bishop's effigy are interlocked in the most complex manner. This may explain why, though Wilson had a workshop in Kent, he sculpted his figures in Venice, and had them cast there by Munaretti of Murano. In *The Stones of Venice,* John Ruskin, patron saint of the Arts and Crafts movement, had argued for the importance of absorbing the lessons of that most beautiful city. Wilson, who had never made much money, may have wanted to spend time there and was unscrupulous about doing so at Aberdeen's expense. On the other hand, Italy certainly led the world in the casting of bronze sculpture, and the monument was a dauntingly complex project.

The chapel committee finally received notice that the bronzes were complete (and

that they were expected to pay for them) in 1931, more than twenty years after the project was first thought of and eighteen years after Wilson's deadline for completing it. It is all too easy to see why they insisted, against Wilson's vehement objections, on having the suite of sculptures shipped directly to Aberdeen. Who knows when (or even if) they would have reappeared if Wilson had been allowed to get his hands on them. The local artist and architect James Cromar Watt, a member of the committee, undertook the complex task of piecing the elements together into a single structure.

The next disagreeable surprise which awaited the committee was the discovery that Wilson, entirely focused on his artistic vision, had forgotten, or dismissed as irrelevant, the stipulation that the new monument should be the same size as the existing tomb. The monument was

undoubtedly fine, but it was also enormous. There was no room for it on the original site. It was put in the ante-chapel for fifteen years, where it was horribly in the way, and in 1946, when the ante-chapel was redesigned as a memorial to the 524 members of the college who died in the World Wars, it was removed to its present place of exile on the lawn.

The monument, though its story has elements of comedy, is in many ways a worthy memorial for the great bishop. Elphinstone lies on his bier, on cushions pattered with the lion of Scotland. On the south side, four Virtues each sit on a corresponding vice: Wisdom on Folly, Hope on Despair, Love on Hatred, Faith on Infidelity. The interactions of the figures are complex and dramatic. Wisdom warns Hope not to draw his sword too quickly; Love appeals to Faith, who responds tenderly. Similarly on the north side,

Prudence sits on Rebellion; Justice on Injustice and Ignorance; Temperance subdues and muzzles the dragon of Licentiousness; and finally, Fortitude conquers Suffering. For all the complexities of the scheme when viewed at close quarters, the overall effect is rich and calm. One touch which would have displeased Elphinstone himself is that whereas the inscription on the tomb in King's is in Latin, the universal language of the Church, that on Wilson's monument is in Gaelic; a well-intentioned gesture, but not, for all that, a particularly appropriate one. Whereas some proportion of the students from earliest times onwards would have understood that language, it was the business of a Renaissance university to turn its students into citizens of the world. Gaelic would have been no more welcome in Elphinstone's quadrangle than Scots.

CHAPTER FOUR

Citizens and Academics

Bishop Elphinstone's vision for his university was an egalitarian one. It was to open a way to talent, as well as to provide the king with an educated, literate nobility: for which the bishop, as a part-time royal servant, knew the need better than most. The Scotland of James IV (r. 1488–1513) was in some of its aspects still a medieval society given to feuding and reiving, and in others, more and more affected by the Renaissance. Great feudal magnates such as the earls of Huntly increasingly lived in a wider world; they began to see the benefits of having heirs who were able to speak French, read Latin, and understand the law, even though they still needed to be able to ride hard and fight fiercely.

The founders of King's envisaged that its students would be drawn from 'princes and the upper nobility' and 'the lower rank of nobility', but would also include the sons of 'farmers, ordinary persons and craftsmen', and even 'those who are prevented by indigence from enjoying a good education'. Bursaries were set up to enable such students to take a well-earned place beside the sons of the better off, and competition was fierce. Fees were set by social class. The upper nobility paid £6 per year and the lower nobility £4, while farmers, merchants and craftsmen could educate their sons for only £2. Thus the

wealthier members of the community subsidised the less well off, a principle which was still being applied as late as the eighteenth century.

'Vultis Lumen?'

The university's early students were worked extremely hard. They got up at five, wakened by the sacrist's bell, and their lectures began at 6 a.m. They spent anything up to ten hours a day in the classroom. They were also locked into the college at night, though it would be a poor body of students that didn't establish a few unofficial exits and the wall was not of a height to defy their ingenuity. But there were also very few of them, so even if the more daring managed the odd night of illicit drinking in town, absence from the morning's classes would not go unobserved. According to Bishop Elphinstone's original constitution of 1504, there were five students in theology, and thirteen in humanities; in 1514, this was revised upwards, and four more boys came to join them. The minute size of the college is an indirect witness to the undeveloped state of the economy, for an output of twenty or so trained professionals a year was sufficient to fulfil the work opportunities that

President of the medical board in Bombay, John Milne MD donated staggering sums for the improvement of education at all levels in his native Aberdeen and Aberdeenshire. The exact date of this portrait by John Moir is unknown, but both men were born in 1775.

Opposite. Seaton Park as it meets the St Machar kirkyard boundary wall.

The silver beaker donated to King's College by Andrew Thomson, who had brought it with him from his home in Danzig (modern Gdansk, Poland) when he came to attend the university in 1642/3.

October, with examinations. Would-be students faced an enquiry into their Latin proficiency, their conduct and their solvency, and existing students were examined to see if they were fit to proceed into the next class. After a fortnight of exams, teaching then began on the 15 October through to July. The first-year students spent the first five months of study on intensive Latin, and from March they began Greek. They had a games afternoon three times a week but otherwise life was a fairly grim round of classes. There were no vacations, so that 'no loss be incurred to either morals or letters by the interruption of studies'. Elphinstone favoured the traditional, though already old-fashioned, practice of 'regenting': a single master took each student through the four years of his course. With a dull master, or any kind of personality clash between teacher and pupil, this must have been just about intolerable, though on the other hand, where the relationship was a good one, it laid the basis for lifelong friendships. Common experience and adversity also forged strong relationships among the students: four years of class-fellowship, declared William Lauder to his classmates during their graduation ceremonies, had forged an unbreakable bond.

In this early period, students were expected to take down the morning's lecture and memorise it, revising it through group work: they met together at eleven, and spent the following hour going over their work in groups while the professors strolled about in their midst checking that they were, in fact, working and not gossiping. At the end of the day, the master tested the class on the contents of the lecture for ninety minutes. The students also spent an hour a day on composition, and they worked on declamation and disputation, skills equally

northern Scotland presented at the time.

The most fundamental thing the boys worked on was languages. Scots was not to be used within the college: students were to communicate, even with one another, in Latin or French. The former was usual in universities; the latter was a language Elphinstone loved for itself and which, because of the Auld Alliance between Scotland and France, he was eager to promote. The first words spoken on a dark winter morning tended to be *vultis lumen?*: 'Do you want a light?' The academic year began on 1

essential to a career in public life, the church, or teaching.

One thing that will be clear from the details of this régime is that the early students had little need for books other than their own notebooks, crammed with material taken down from dictation. From the beginning, the size and richness of the college library was remarkable for so small a foundation and was constantly augmented, but it was only indirectly for the benefit of the student body.

Idle or half-hearted students who failed to memorise their lectures were scolded, and if they did not mend their ways they were expelled. Of the fifteen students who entered the class of 1611, only eight made it to graduation. But there were also many punishments which fell short of actual expulsion, suggesting that virtue did not reign supreme, at least, not all the time. Those who were absent without leave, used abusive language, talked profanely, sang vulgar songs, played ball games in the courtyard, or otherwise misbehaved were punished by a fine or by blows on the palm of the hand: a form of corporal punishment that remained part of Scottish school life into the twentieth century and was only outlawed in the 1980s. On games after-noons students were herded down to the links, by the shore, to play football; they were accom-panied by a master to ensure that none of them doubled back to sample such dissipation as the town offered. The university Visitation of 1549, aware that the college bought in its bread and some of its beer from the town, recommended that no female brewers or bakers should enter the college and, similarly, that women who attended services in the chapel should not enter it via the college gates, but by the main door. They were clearly determined to keep chat-up

While Thomson was probably of Scottish parentage, the origins of his classmate and travelling companion, Peter Specht, are harder to discern. Specht also donated a beaker, seen here.

opportunities to a minimum. Similarly, students were forbidden to wear armour or carry weapons, however blue their blood, even though in normal circumstances a gentleman expected to wear a sword and be prepared to use it.

King's students were recruited primarily from Scotland's North and North-east. The oldest universities of Europe, such as Paris and Bologna, organised their students into 'nations' based on their place of origin, and this was imitated at Aberdeen (as well as Glasgow and St Andrews, both of which were also founded in the fifteenth century). But at King's, the 'nations' were merely districts of northern Scotland: Mar, Buchan, Moray and Angus. Would-be students from the Lowlands found it more convenient to go to Glasgow or St Andrews, and no outright foreigners – from England or anywhere else – are found until the seventeenth century.

Student Life: Reformation to Revolution

King's, like Glasgow and St Andrews, was overhauled to make it fit for the purposes of a newly Protestant kingdom in the later sixteenth century. But at every major turn in Scottish history, King's College may be found stubbornly clinging to the old ways, and the Reformation was no exception. Andrew Melville, one of the greatest scholars of Reformation-era Scotland, revised the curriculum of his own university, Glasgow, in 1577 and that of St Andrews in 1579. By contrast, when the New Foundation scheme was raised at King's – for the second time – in 1597, it failed to meet with formal approval, though some elements of reform were adopted. King's continued to employ the by-then archaic system of having one professor teach everything to a given cohort of students rather than allowing them to specialise. Under cover of the 'New Foundation', the principal and the surviving four professors attempted to allow the two legal professorships, of canon (Church) and civil law, and the professorship of medicine to die with their incumbents. Only theology and humanities were taught, a considerable simplification of their commitments, though the Visitations of 1619 and 1638 put a spoke in the regents' wheel, and insisted that the posts of

civilist, canonist and mediciner should be reinstated.

The slimming of the curriculum may be connected with the fact that there were many more students than the original foundation had envisaged, and the teaching load was consequently getting heavier. Early seventeenth-century King's offered twelve bursaries, awarded competitively, but by the end of the century, there were up to thirty-six. Numbers in general were rising: by 1645, there were sixty-four students in college; thirty years later, there were 143. Pressure on space was considerable. In 1604, the principal himself was forced to give up one of his own rooms to 'the Maister of Ogilvie his sonnis vith their pedagogue'. Students lived three to a room, and paid ten shillings a year for the privilege, in addition to charges for board and for cleaning. They were well fed, and except for Lent and the 'fish days' of Friday and Saturday, they expected to see meat on the table every evening; beef, mutton, chicken, or salt beef. Interestingly, though pigs were kept in Old Aberdeen (periodically they escaped into other people's gardens and wrought a havoc reflected in the records), pork and bacon are not mentioned in the accounts. A variety of travellers in northern Scotland observed that the natives had a strong aversion to pork as late as the eighteenth century. John Lesley, bishop of Ross, mentions in his *History of Scotland*, written in the 1570s, that 'our cuntrie peple' have 'lytle plesure' in pork. This taboo was either felt at King's, or observed in deference to the sensibilities of Highland students. Otherwise, there was generally plenty of fish to be had, both fresh and salted; the college brewed its own ale and grew its own vegetables, though butter, milk and white bread were still bought in from the

Seventeenth-century King's students were marked off from the local populace by their distinctive red gowns.

townsfolk. The scholarship boys lived more humbly: the college brewed both 'bursar aill' and 'best aill', and baked 'bursar bread' out of oatmeal. The first-year bursars had two rooms, containing seven beds, between the twelve of them.

Despite the crying need for accommodation, new building works could not be undertaken due to lack of funds. In the 1640s, Principal William Guild re-roofed the privies, but it was another twenty years before new teaching and accommodation blocks could be built. A stone structure, still standing and now called the Cromwell Tower, went up in the 1660s, together with a wooden block called the Timber Muses which lasted for 200 years. Before then it was unavoidable that students slept three to a room, and often two to a bed. Even after the seventeenth century's new construction, increased student numbers and gradually rising standards of comfort and privacy ensured that the accommodation crisis was continuous. Well-born, or simply rich students rented single chambers if they could, though since the dignity of even a youthful nobleman had to be supported by a retinue, this was no guarantee of privacy. Hugh Rose, for example, had a chamber, but he also imported his tutor and his page; so although he had chosen his company, he was sleeping three to a room like most of the others. But a new aspect of student life in the seventeenth century was that an increasing number lived in lodgings in the town. Thus the academic community became less introverted and more directly involved with the life of the burgh.

Details about individual students record a socially mixed group, just as the founder had envisaged. The four sons of George, second marquis of Huntly, were students at King's, as were other boys from the landed gentry: Urquhart, for example, and James Crichton of Frendraught. But many of their fellows were the sons of poor men.

Another aspect of early student life at Aberdeen which would now seem surprising is how young some of the scholars were. Seventeenth-century King's had a separate grammar school at the door. This school dated from the Reformation, after which it took over the business of basic Latin education from the cathedral choir-school in the Chanonry, but status, or some other consideration now unrecoverable, seems to have militated against sending young noblemen there. It is not easy to demonstrate, since matriculation records do not give a student's age at entrance, but there seems to be a distinct correlation between extreme youth and gentry or noble status. Thomas Urquhart, future mathematician, author, translator, royalist soldier and laird of Cromarty, was just eleven when he came to King's in 1622.

By the seventeenth century there were clearly concessions to the principle that well-born students needed to acquire gentlemanly accomplishments such as golf, bowls, and archery, as well as Latin. In 1636–37, Simon Fraser, from a family very important in Aberdeenshire, distinguished himself at 'ballown, cachpole, byars, bowles, the goffe, and arching'.

The result was that the King's community became a two-tier one. Well-bred little boys were subjected to as much discipline and learning as they were capable of absorbing, while permitted considerably more entertainment than the statutes enjoined, to judge by Simon Fraser's list of sporting accomplishments. Seventeenth-century records suggest that it was getting harder and harder for the authorities to insist that Latin, not Scots, was spoken, a problem which must have been made worse by the presence of these youngsters. At the same time, bursary-holders and the sons of merchants, ministers and the like were older boys who hoped to enter one of the learned professions, and who were aware that their future depended on their diligence. They slogged through the punishing régime of lectures and classes enjoined upon them, disputing, making Latin verses, and learning their lecture notes just as their predecessors had done. A number of well-born boys arrived accompanied by a 'pedagogue', or personal tutor-cum-minder, indicating that the university authorities recognised that children needed rather different treatment from young adults. This is not to suggest, however, that all the young nobles were idlers. George Mackenzie, first earl of Cromarty (1630–1714), was a man of immensely wide intellectual interests, who became not only a politician, but also a naturalist, geographer, historian, and theologian.

Apart from young nobles using King's as a Scottish equivalent of Eton, the seventeenth-century student body included a respectable number who went on to make a distinguished name for themselves. They include John Leech who entered King's in 1610, graduating MA in 1614, and became a noted and extremely prolific Latin poet before meeting a bizarre end, recorded in a news pamphlet of 1662: he was allegedly 'carried twelve miles in the ayre by two furies' – perhaps the victim of a tornado. Another King's graduate who died violently was James Sharp, a churchman and scholar who was, in his capacity as archbishop of St Andrews, dragged from his coach on Magus Moor and murdered by Covenanters in 1679. Another alumnus, William Leslie, a great-grandnephew of William Elphinstone, ended his days more comfortably as 'Bishop of Laybach, Metropolitan of Carniola, betwixt Vienna and Venice, Privy Councillor to his Imperial Majesty'.

The Union of the Crowns in 1603 promoted a new kind of interaction between Scotland and England. Sixteenth-century Aberdeen students were by no means unadventurous, with individuals making their lives in France, Scandinavia, or even further afield, but they did not venture south of Hadrian's Wall. This changed in the seventeenth century. Leech, who lived mostly in England after 1617, was not the only alumnus to make his career in the South: one of the most distinguished to do so was James Fraser, a passionate bibliophile and book dealer, who became librarian to Charles II, and bequeathed to King's a number of its greatest treasures. English scholars came to Aberdeen occasionally, the first in 1633. One of them, another bibliophile called Edward Baynard, may have given the college authorities quite a lot of trouble, since he had a hair-trigger temper. Later in life he was admonished for calling the president of the Royal College of Physicians 'the son of A Whore'. Thomas Beverley, who graduated from King's in 1643, became an independent minister and took to prophesying the end of the world, so may have caused trouble of a very different kind. Henry Jenkes, who became a senior scholar of Gonville and Caius College in Cambridge, was less erratic in his learning. A solitary student in the class of 1663, 'Patricius Galatheu, Burdigalensis', came from even further away: Burdigala is the Latin for Bordeaux. His presence is a reminder of important trading links: claret was the drink par excellence of Highland nobility and gentry (whisky then being for the lower orders), and there was a small Scottish colony of dealers and shippers in France to facilitate the trade.

Despite the college's best attempts to ensure that 'none shall be admitted to [King's], none maintained there, in whom there is no sign of modesty or diligence', there were more than a few students in whom either modesty or diligence were far to seek. Some were spectacularly lawless. Although students were absolutely, and repeatedly, forbidden to go armed, in 1665 a group of King's lads, 'drawing their swords and shooting their pistolls', helped the son of a local laird to abduct a woman from St Machar's Kirk one Sunday. Others got drunk or fornicated. In 1705, four King's students even collaborated to free a man imprisoned in the town tollbooth: 'they broke the floore . . . and helped the prisoner up through the hole they had made.'

The authorities were particularly wary of collective student activity, which frequently led to trouble. Rivalry between the King's students

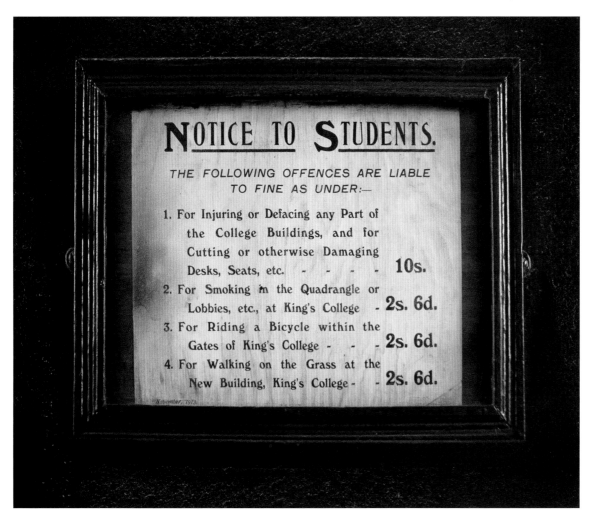

of Old Aberdeen and the students of Marischal College in New Aberdeen sometimes led to major affrays in which bands of twenty or thirty students fought with clubs and knives; a number were hurt, though none was ever killed. There were other occasions of collective horseplay, sanctioned by tradition: the most annoying of which was the end-of-year free-for-all known as 'chalking the schools' – covering doors and walls with graffiti (see box, p.138). It might have been overlooked if it had been merely a matter of chalk, but 'chalking' spread out of the college, and students started decorating the doors and gates of the townsfolk. It continued to escalate into an occasion for general vandalism. Locks and even doors got broken; so did windows. Principal Guild legislated against 'chalking' in 1641, and by the early 1670s students had to sign an undertaking that they would not participate in 'chalking', on pain of expulsion. However, the practice may have been rather more in the nature of an ancient privilege than an annoying seventeenth-century fad. Some of the oldest educational institutions in Europe,

King's Chapel's Early-modern Graffiti

Only a handful of the original late-medieval seats and bench-ends in King's Chapel are without carved student graffiti of some kind. Almost all of it dates from the late sixteenth to the early nineteenth century, with a significant gap in the first half of the 1700s. Far too plentiful to be catalogued exhaustively here, it ranges in quality from tiny scratches, barely discernible as lettering without the aid of a strong light, to complete names (with and without dates) such as 'IOA:OGSTOUN:1.5.8.2', to whole groups of kinsmen and elaborate heraldic devices. Later 'work' tends to include places of origin, presumably added for clarity as the student body grew but the region's stock of surnames did not, hence: 'ALEXR FALCONER FROM EDD', 'WILM GRAY FROM T', 'I MALCOLMSON FROM G', and 'A † SMITH ELGIN'. Highland surnames are also frequently seen, with at least one Campbell joining 'GEO. H. MCDONELL', 'IOHN MACRA 1779', and a very large 'RORIE MAKENZIE' dated 21 March 1645. One probably Welsh name, 'I. IENKINS', can also be seen, carved within its own decorative border, on the east end of the choir stalls.

Smith from Elgin was not the only student to include a pictorial device with his name. To separate their first from last names, most used a colon, but Thomas Molysson used a heart and John Forbes a pentagram, while 'GVLL [William] GORDON' began both his names with a single enormous G that also enclosed the date, 1610. Another boy placed three crosses after his surname. On the second seat from the west end of the north wall, a student has carved a complete armorial shield with the fess chequy device common to the Stewarts, Lindsays, Boyds and other prominent families. Though it is impossible to identify for certain due to the absence of colour, three small birds above the fess suggest it may be the arms of the Houstons of Houston. 'ADAM G' appears within a shield shape, and on the rood screen itself, we also find a Maltese cross inscribed in a circle.

The bravado of the illicit carvers varied

greatly. 'VIL:ZOVNG' – Will Young – seems to be the only student to have carved his name on the rood screen's doors, though others somehow got inside the screen and carved their names there. The 'FRAT=RES', brothers, H. Gordon, A. Gordon and P. Gordon, inscribed their names not merely large and deeply, but nearly seven feet off the floor. Andrew Abercrombie got up even higher, while the aforementioned Smith of Elgin and Rorie Makenzie must have stood on the seat backs, if not ladders, to carve their names where they did. Frequency rather than aerobatics was the forte of some students: 'IA. ANDERSONE MAIOR 1610' and 'ALEXR. BIRNIE 1801' occur in almost identical form twice each, while

Molysson signed his name at least four times in a variety of styles (and spellings). For sheer size, it would be difficult to beat 'IOHN SANDILANDS 1632' or 'ROBERT VDNY 1654', though 'VILLIAME FRASER' must be commended for centring his name so precisely, one letter per fold of the linen-fold panelling on the back of his seat, third from the altar end of the north inside tier.

Kinship groups could be like the Gordon brothers, or trans-generational: thus we find '1625 APRYL 9 HVGO IRVIN' immediately above 'PA:IRVING ANNO DO 1586'. Both, like many others in the chapel, are of a quality with the carving on gravestones of similar dates. Ligatures, the joining of one letter to the next, are very

frequent, for instance the 'NE' in 'ANDERSONE' and both pairs of 'ND' in 'SANDILANDS'. In 'DAVID SIBBALD 1614', the 'AVI' is rendered using just four strokes. Fear of getting caught no doubt led to some corners being cut, but these unexpected ligatures only add to the individuality and charm of each monogram.

Because the carving appears to have been stopped altogether in or shortly after 1820, no female students' names appear, but that is not to say that no women are mentioned. In the south upper deck of the choir stalls, with a straightforward symbolism recognisable to writers and readers of graffiti everywhere, we find that IA♥AD.

Opposite. Eighteenth-century caricature of the King's College academic staff, variously depicted as a Highland rebel, Death, and the Pope.

notably the University of Salamanca (founded 1218) and Westminster School (with its origins in the twelfth century), permitted graduates to paint or carve their names. The façade of Salamanca and the seventeenth-century gateway to 'School' bear witness to the custom to this day, though perhaps the only institution still to perpetuate it is the University of Leiden where, even now, graduates write their name on the walls of the 'Zweetkamertje'. Unfortunately, rivalry between 'nations' – or individuals – or a developing fashion for bigger and better can easily and rapidly lead to such a tradition getting completely out of hand, as clearly it did in Old Aberdeen.

Just as problems generated by religion created havoc in the King's of the sixteenth century, college life in the seventeenth century was inevitably affected by the series of political catastrophes which engulfed the nation. George Gordon, marquis of Huntly, leader of the most politically important Catholic family in Scotland and a thorn in the flesh of the Kirk, sent two sons to King's in 1630, and their presence alone ensured that the university could not stay out of politics. The marquis, after all, had been ordered by the Privy Council to send them to St Andrews or Cambridge to ensure that their upbringing was sufficiently Protestant. His defiance of this order suggests that King's was far more tolerant than the Kirk enjoined. This is confirmed by the events of 1638, when the principal, John Leslie, and five other doctors of divinity refused to sign the National Covenant, and led the national resistance to it. It took the marquis of Montrose arriving with an army to make Old Aberdeen capitulate on this issue, even after which Principal Leslie and two others refused to sign and had to be removed from office.

Three years later, following the abolition of the office of bishop in the Scots Kirk, the General Assembly of the Church of Scotland proposed that episcopal revenues should be used to support education. Charles I was glad to agree, since it was a gesture of conciliation towards Scotland which cost him nothing. Two-thirds of the revenues of the bishop of Aberdeen went to King's, and the rest to Marischal. Charles also beautified King's Chapel with a small and graceful central spire, which still adorns it. Less acceptably, given the intense rivalry between King's and Marischal, he decreed that the two should be, for all time to come, a single unit: King Charles's University of Aberdeen.

In 1649, the year in which Charles I was executed in London, King's underwent another ideological purge. The General Assembly deposed the principal, William Guild, the sub-principal, Alexander Middleton, and two of the regents, as being 'malignants', a common term of abuse for those with royalist leanings. But the Kirk failed to agree on a new principal and Guild was reinstated, only to be ejected once more in 1651 when Scotland passed under the rule of an occupying English army and English commissioners ensured that the universities were governed by men acceptable to the new regime. After the Restoration, the shotgun wedding between King's and Marischal was dissolved, Episcopacy was restored, and the bishop of Aberdeen once more became chancellor. John Row, an austere Presbyterian scholar of Hebrew who had been put in Guild's place, was deposed in his turn and replaced by Middleton.

The effect of all this on the student body is hard to determine. James Fraser, for example, loved the college as it was at mid-century, and felt it had done well by him. He called his regent,

The Sapient Septemviri

1 The Beauty of Holiness, Lecturing.

2 Had you not sold your Patronages, First Minister might have been annexed to my Divine Chair of Verity & taste.

3 Annually for 45 years and upwards have I beat up, even to the Ultima Thule have I recruited our University.

4 I have rendered Vernacular the Greek Language from Aberdour to Aberdeen.

5 Agriculture is the Noblest of Sciences, mind your Glebes, the Emperor of China is a Farmer.

6 Has not the Effulgence of my Countenance been a light unto your feet, and a lamp unto your Paths.

7 Colledge property, Patronages are unalienable, so says the Law, the Noble Patron has rewarded most justly your Rapacity.

8 Degrees Male and Female in Medicine and Midwifery, sold here for ready money.

John Strachan, 'one of the greate humanists and Philosophs of the Kingdom. Under his hand and government I myselfe spent my 4 yeares in the Kings Colledge, my deare and indulgent Master'. At the same time, Fraser spoke bitterly of other masters who were forced upon the college by 'the swaying faction of the English and Sectarians of the Kingdom', and other respected professors who were thrust out to make room for them. The sense of 'a world turned upside down' may well have been a factor in their bad behaviour: in particular, the forced amalgamation of the 1640s seems if anything to have intensified rivalry between the two colleges.

Compared to the dramas that attended King's involvements with the politics of the mid-century, the effects of the 1688–89 Revolution which deposed James VII and brought William and Mary to the throne were surprisingly minimal. Only one King's academic, the pioneering archaeologist and professor of divinity, James Garden, refused to subscribe to the Confession of Faith or swear allegiance to the new monarchs; even he was not removed until 1697.

The Jacobite Years

One aspect of university life which changed quite radically over the course of the eighteenth century was that students increasingly got their knowledge from books. They spent less and less time in the classroom, and lectures were no longer the be-all and end-all. The richer students bought their books; bizarrely, the King's authorities forbade students to attend the New Town book auction in 1765. Their rationale was that this was yet another mode of student extrava-

gance, 'purchasing unnecessary Books ... [and] thereafter stating it to their Parents and Friends as money necessarily expended on their Education', thus 'tending to raise unreasonable clamour, as if the Education was expensive'. Instead, in a new development, students were allowed to borrow books from the university library, on payment of a returnable deposit (£1, enough to keep the poorer students out). In earlier periods students were required to make a contribution to the library, but there is little or no indication that they used it themselves. The importance of the King's library in the eighteenth century is shown by the fact that books were no longer accrued randomly as bequests: the library's collection was augmented in a fairly organised fashion with new stock from Stationers' Hall. One student from England, George Colman, who had been sent up to Aberdeen as 'an academical Penitentiary' by his exasperated father because he had been wasting his time at Oxford, became a regular user, and came to enjoy the world of books. The library he browsed in was housed at that time in the west end of the chapel, which had ceased to be used for its original purpose after the Reformation.

There was a major curriculum reform in 1753–54, masterminded by the philosopher Thomas Reid. King's eliminated the last vestiges of the Greek and Latin curriculum of earlier centuries, and put in place a course which covered beginner's Greek, Latin, classical history, and – a new development – English in the first year, elementary mathematics and history in the second, advanced mathematics and physics in the third, and moral philosophy with logic in the fourth. This curriculum, Reid argued, would be both rational and useful. Despite this formidable-sounding list of subjects, students spent

Opposite. James Mackay Hall, King's College, long occupied by the university arts library.

only about three hours attending lectures each day, and so extra-curricular teaching and learning became increasingly important. Seventeenth-century students would hardly have had the hours to spare, but the increasing laxity of the official curriculum meant that students were far more free to follow their interests. John Munro, who came to King's in 1719, learned French, dancing and the flute alongside his formal studies. In 1753, the increasing importance of 'polite learning' was formally acknowledged by the authorities, who recommended suitable teachers, and even allowed them to teach on the premises. By 1763, a very good drawing-master (who also taught French) had a room in college. Those who were more genuinely academic in their leanings also turned to private tuition to make up for the deficiencies of the lectures. Most students needed help with their Greek. By the 1770s, English had finally won out as the language of instruction for all the subjects but one: Greek continued to be taught in Latin. This would have raised considerable problems for those students whose Latin was on the shaky side – a good three-quarters of them, or so their professor thought.

Increasingly, students lived outside the university's walls. In 1730, the authorities took alarm at this diaspora, and insisted that the twenty-four bursars all live in the college, sweetening the pill by accommodating them rent-free. Very few fee-paying students chose to join them. By 1780, the college had taken over Old Aberdeen to the extent that it could be claimed that 'most of the Inhabitants live by letting Rooms to Students'. Some careful parents seem to have thought in terms of taking a house in the burgh for the duration of their boys' education. In 1738 it was noted that, since the burgh did

not boast 'an accomplished gentlewoman for teaching white and coloured seam', several gentlemen's sons were educated elsewhere, 'their parents inclining to send them where they might have suitable education for their daughters also'. The university took this sufficiently seriously as an aspect of its overall competitiveness, and advanced £12 to a suitably accomplished gentlewoman called May Cuthbert, who also received £20 from the council.

Accommodation had always been a major problem at King's, but students who lived out in the town were far less easy to police, a matter for additional concern. The official sports afternoons of the college's early days had fallen into abeyance, but with students scattered all over the town and so few lectures, they were hardly necessary. Students were more than equal to the challenge of finding leisure-time activities. Apart from finding time to study French, dancing and the flute, John Munro fenced, played golf, and went riding. Quite a number of students rode for their recreation; there may have been someone in the town who hired out horses. Around 1725 there was another burst of building: the ruinous south block of the original quadrangle, which had been given over to student housing, was taken down and replaced with a more multi-purpose structure which included a social space known as the Lobby. Many of the students loved to dance, and did so in the Lobby, to the music of a fiddle. In the eighteenth century these dances were mixed. For the first time in its history, girls were coming into the university, and trouble came with them: it was rumoured that some students were contriving to have sex with their dance partners in nooks and corners of the college, so the regents therefore put a stop to it. Highland students, however, would continue to

hold bachelor ceilidhs, and dance with each other. Their fiddler was John Ross, a very skilful blind musician who lived in the Spital.

The age witnessed a new concern with politeness, but loutish behaviour continued to be very much part of student life. There were riots at King's in 1728 and 1781. The best that could be said about the reform of manners is that student warfare tended to involve snowballs rather than edged weapons. Pryse Gordon, who came to the college in 1776, threw one at the sacrist and inadvertently hit a professor. He was fined five shillings. Another tiresome new fad which developed in the late eighteenth century, and was repeatedly prohibited, was ripping other people's gowns: not easy to prevent, when every student had to carry a sharp little penknife for mending his quills. A gown could be an expensive item; Lord George Hay paid £2 16s 8d for his.

Long intensive days of study had previously forged close relationships between students in the same year. This was decreasingly the case as students spent fewer hours herded together and more time on private pursuits of all kinds. There was tension between bursary-holders and fee-payers. Pryse Gordon, a bursar, noted that 'the sons of the richer lairds, or private gentlemen, look down on the poor bursars and treat them with contempt', a contempt which was returned by those of the bursars who viewed the wealthier boys as 'libertines' or dilettantes. Sometimes there were tensions between Highlanders and Lowlanders, and it seems more than likely that the political troubles of the eighteenth century were felt at student level.

One purely personal rivalry emerged into verse: there seems to have been a love-affair at the bottom of it, but what actually survives are elaborate insults and counter-insults which became an end in themselves. One of the combatants was James Ogilvie, and the little book is called *The Ogilviad: a heroic poem, being a dispute between two gentlemen of King's College* (Aberdeen, 1789). In a typical passage, the anonymous challenger accuses Ogilvy of wearing hand-me-downs from his grandfather:

> *The hero's dress I'll now describe*
> *But not by any means deride;*
> *With sky-blue ribbons decking both*
>   *his knees,*
> *He proudly struts with unaffected ease.*
> *The tiny buttons his green coat adorn*
> *That by his sires in former times was worn.*
> *The coat itself was bought at second hand*
> *And half a crown was the immense*
>   *demand;*
> *The boots, an ornament to him not mean*
> *Their fiftieth year, I'm confident, have seen.*

There must have been enough truth in the old-fashionedness of his appearance for this to sting – though he was probably not the only King's student to have second-hand items in his wardrobe. However, young Ogilvy gave as good as he got to his anonymous foe, and the wordy battle must have mightily amused the friends (and enemies) of both parties.

One reflection of the lack of cohesiveness among the King's students of the late eighteenth century was the gradual demise of the college table. There were, in fact, two tables, and always had been; the bursars at the second table getting cheaper and plainer food. As fewer and fewer students lived in, the common dinner became less important. Towards the end of the eighteenth century even those who lived in

Opposite. Burgh houses and King's College, with the North Sea visible in the distance. Painted by Francis Oliver Finch.

frequently ate in their rooms, and by 1799 the 'public table' was said to have been abolished 'for some time'.

Reid's concept of academic education was a generalist training of the mind, and the products suggest that he was not unsuccessful in his aims. One student, James Mackintosh, summed up the experience: 'I quitted college with little regular and exact knowledge, but with considerable activity of mind.' Alongside the inevitable crop of theologians and classicists, the livelier King's alumni of the eighteenth century included James Burnett, Lord Monboddo, a philosopher who wrote a groundbreaking study on the origins of language and achieved an international reputation as a speculative thinker. George Colman, that keen browser in the library, wrote two plays, *The Female Dramatist* and *Two for One*, during his sojourn in Old Aberdeen, both of which were put on in London; the second, though not the first, was a success. Colman went on to manage the Haymarket Theatre, and to produce hit after hit in Regency London. Joseph Forsyth, smitten by Roman antiquities in the first year of his studies, visited Italy and wrote on Italian art and history. George Halket, Jacobite songwriter, had the courage of his political convictions – as, in his way, did the notorious traitor, Simon Fraser, Lord Lovat.

Union with Marischal and Beyond

By the nineteenth century, King's and Marischal had agreed to divide their concerns. Students of science and medicine were taught at Marischal College in the New Town, so for the students of King's remained law, humanities, or divinity. However, the colleges were not formally united into a single university until 1857, after much argument. 'The paper war of the "fusionists" and the "anti-fusionists" raged for years,' as William Walker, nineteenth-century historian of Aberdeen's literary life, vividly expressed it, 'the brisk musketry rattle of newspaper correspondence was varied by big booms from the editorial ordnance, and the frequent rushing hiss of the pamphleteer's shell.'

The legend of nineteenth-century Aberdeen, as it was developed by the authors of a series of university novels, implies that many of its students were drawn 'from the plough's tail', labourers, or crofters, living all term on a barrel of oatmeal brought from home. Like so many legends it has a grain of truth in it, but the majority of Aberdeen students came from middle-class homes, the sons of country ministers, schoolmasters, small businessmen, modest farmers. Especially in cases where the parental home teemed with children, students were often getting by on very little and their pleasures had to be inexpensive, but they were not as spectacularly poverty-stricken as fictions like *Life in a Northern University* imply. However, it was still true to say that Aberdeen opened up opportunities for the less well-off. Both in terms of fees and cost of living, the university was one of the cheapest places to get a higher education in the English-speaking world, especially for bursary-holders. In 1852, a royal commission found that the annual cost of student life in Aberdeen was less than one twenty-fifth that of Oxford, that is, £12 as against £300. Half a century later, Sir Herbert Grierson, professor of English Literature at Aberdeen and the father of five talented daughters, could afford to send only one of them to Oxford. All five could have gone to Aberdeen for the same money.

Another aspect of Aberdeen and the other old Scottish universities little remembered today is that they were the first to offer degrees to black students at a time when American universities applied a colour bar and before the foundation of Howard as a black university. Few early-nineteenth-century black men living in Europe or the USA were in easy financial circumstances, so black would-be students were almost invariably struggling financially. A Scottish university degree was the best value for money then obtainable. Beyond that, the fact that students lived in lodgings where they were fed by their landladies, and that there was far less emphasis on social interaction, let alone social exclusion, than at Oxford or Cambridge, made it much easier for black students to fit in. The university authorities were concerned that their intake should be good Protestants, but this was the only form of barrier they applied. Black students were not numerous in Aberdeen, but they were a reminder of a wider world. Some showed extraordinary determination and made their own mark. Perhaps the most remarkable was Christopher James Davis, a black Barbadian who studied medicine at Aberdeen, became house physician at St Bartholomew's Hospital in London, and selflessly journeyed to France during the Franco-Prussian War to help the fever-stricken and starving peasants. He died of smallpox there.

The students were a highly visible part of the Old Aberdeen world. They still wore the *toga rubra*, or red gown, first mentioned in the mid-seventeenth century. As so often with compulsory garments, a new-looking gown was a garment of shame, and a faded, shredded one the only possible wear. Gowns made their first appearance on the first Sunday of the term, and

Offices modern and ancient in the History of Art department.

Opposite. King's College Chapel has always been a favoured backdrop for student photographs.

rough horseplay on the Lord's Day would have brought down the wrath of the authorities. But the following Monday was 'tearing day', when second- and third-year students ('semis' and 'tertians', in Aberdeen parlance) set on the 'bajans', or first years, and did as much damage to their new gowns as possible: a formalisation of the sly gown-slashing which had been such a nuisance in earlier times.

Regardless of the nuances of gown-wearing within the student community, any red gown at all was a red rag to the local children. Students who lodged in the Spital, if they were brave enough to wear the gown outside college precincts, were jeered as they trudged to their lectures with the song:

> They took a man and killed him deid
> And stapped him in a holie,
> Buttery Wullie, Buttery Wullie,
> Buttery Wullie Colie!

Willie Collie was a well-known street trader of the mid-nineteenth century, the local equivalent of a 'muffin man', since he sold 'butteries', a local variant on the croissant still much loved in Aberdeen. But the line 'killed him deid' suggests a confusion with a legend of the 1780s or earlier: that a group of King's students, 'ragging' a deeply unpopular sacrist named Downie, staged a mock trial and execution, complete with axe, block, and hooded axe-man. When Downie was blindfolded and struck on the neck – with a wet towel – the farce was supposed to end. The problem was, he had actually died, probably of a heart attack. The identities of the students responsible were successfully kept quiet, but for years afterwards, children's taunts would include, 'Airt an' pairt in Downie's slauchter?'

and 'Fa [who] killed Downie?'

Mock executions aside, student 'rags' were not particularly inventive; they stole door knockers, broke street lamps, overturned carts, and generally made a nuisance of themselves much as the students of Oxford and Cambridge did. They had favourite 'howffs', or pubs, one of which was the Red Lion in the Spital, famous a century before as a meeting-place of the Wise Club. In the late nineteenth century it was kept by a Mrs Hay, who hung out a signboard with the Hay family motto, *serva jugum*, 'keep the yoke'. Naturally, the students preferred to translate this as 'serve a jug'. One student malefactor who made himself conspicuous was Alexander Tawse, a large, strong Highlander whose Christmas party in the Old Town in 1812 led to the breaking of windows. Tawse compounded his crimes by holding a more private gathering in a room in college with 'some wenches'. He was deprived of his ten-guinea bursary for roistering, womanising, and for threatening behaviour, but his punishment polarised Highland and Lowland students in the college – the Lowlanders thought he should have been expelled – and tensions ran high for a time.

One of the most dramatic innovations in nineteenth-century King's was the introduction of women who were not 'wenches', but students in their own right. The issue of admitting women was first raised in the 1870s, but got bogged down in university politics. The Scottish universities were empowered to admit women by an act which came into force in 1892. Eleven pioneers came to King's that year, and thereafter numbers gradually increased. Since King's students now almost all lived in lodgings, the presence of women created far less practical difficulty than it did in Oxford and Cambridge, though the men

The Aberdeen Universities Officers Training Corps, 2007.

greeted them with a predictable mixture of facetiousness and alarm. Finding themselves excluded from the existing debating society, female students founded their own. They further demonstrated their independence by refusing to live in the hall of residence created for them, with the best of intentions, at Castleton House in the Chanonry. The fact that it was at a distance from King's and from the sometimes loutish student life of the High Street was significant to the thinking of Lady Geddes, the creator of the

residence, but the women students valued convenience over refined and maidenly seclusion.

Whatever feathers were ruffled in town or college by the presence of women students, the issue was cast into a truer perspective by the calamity of the First World War. Nearly 3,000 alumni served, and 341 were killed. Between 1916 and 1918, women outnumbered men in the university as a whole, and even though the return of the servicemen brought an end to this state of affairs, they had consolidated their

position. It was still a very small university which had only passed the thousand student mark for the first time in 1909. Much of the Middle Toun has since been swallowed by lecture theatres, halls of residence and other university buildings, but by no means all of it has, as witnessed by the environs of the remarkable MacRobert Memorial Garden (see box, p.154). The scurrying students also still co-exist with permanent residents – and probably more amicably than in any previous century.

Student Life Today

The student of today, especially if coming from overseas, will as likely as not first see Aberdeen from the air, perhaps noting that the choice of blue and grey for the city's buses has done little to alleviate the New Town's world-famous monochromatic quality. Exiting the small, grimly efficient airport into light rain, surprisingly cold for mid-September, she will find her way to a taxi, its driver silent and solemn or

The zoology building, an outsized cabinet of curiosities.

Around the MacRobert Memorial Garden

Grant's Place, a row of one-storey pantiled cottages dating to the 1720s, looks like another almshouse, but in fact it is not. Both Grant's Place and the neighbouring, rather later, Wright's and Cooper's Place were restored by the distinguished conservation architects Robert Hurd & Partners for the university, via a gift from the MacRobert Trust in 1965. Both rows were very much worth preserving, and could easily have been swept away. It has taken some time for planners and preservationists to realise that groups of small and modest buildings can be important as well as grand ones. The two Places, with their pretty gardens, add enormously to the charm of Old Aberdeen's High Street and it is worth walking to the end of Wright's and Cooper's Place to find the MacRobert Memorial Garden: secret-looking, but in fact completely open to anyone who comes along, a peaceful space to read or just sit and think.

Lady Rachel MacRobert, née Workman (1880–1954), was born in Worcester, Massachusetts, the daughter of a famous New England physician, and became a remarkable woman in her own right. She took a degree in geology at Imperial College, London, and was one of the first women to be elected a fellow of the Geological Society. In 1911, she married Sir Alexander MacRobert, who was born to an Aberdeen labourer and died as first baronet of Cawnpore and Cromar. He went out to India as the managing director of the Cawnpore (Kanpur) Woollen Mill when he was thirty, and became the founder of the British India Corporation, a successful textile company which is still based in Kanpur. Sir Alexander died in 1922, when their oldest son was only ten, and Rachel MacRobert not only raised her family, but took over as a director of the BIC. She lived to see all three of their sons killed in aeroplanes. The first died in an accident

shortly before the Second World War began, while the second and third were shot down in May and June of 1941. In October of the same year, she wrote a cheque for £25,000 to the RAF for a Stirling Bomber. 'I have no more sons to wear the MacRobert badge or carry it in the fight,' she wrote, 'but if I had ten sons, I know they would all have followed that line of duty.' The plane was named *MacRobert's Reply*, and the MacRobert crest was painted on its nose. She gave a total of six aircraft to the RAF in the course of the war.

Left as a wealthy and childless widow, Lady MacRobert created the MacRobert Trust, which has given lavishly to a variety of causes over the last fifty years, and founded the highly prestigious MacRobert Award, Britain's premier prize for innovation in engineering, before dying peacefully at the family home in 1954. The memorial garden was created in 1965.

chatty, but alas, completely incomprehensible. Along with the vast majority of new arrivals, she will be taken to Hillhead of Seaton.

Essentially a small city unto itself, Hillhead was designed – according to a legend perpetuated by generation after generation of students – as a Swedish prison. (One is also frequently told that Marischal College was Adolf Hitler's favourite building in Europe, and that he planned use it as his primary residence after winning the war.) From every angle, 'Hell Hid' appears dauntingly isolated. It is roughly the northern half of the Hay of Seaton estate, extending from Balgownie village to the site of Seaton House which burned down in 1963 – only the stable block and a small brick-walled garden remain. Despite its almost immediate proximity, most students will never visit

Balgownie with its famous medieval bridge. It is no longer on the way to anywhere: a lost city's lost suburb.

The Hillhead site is roughly square, screened on all sides by tall trees, and on three by the fast-moving River Don. Inevitably, however, the student must tear herself away from the full bar, games rooms, televisions, computers, snack machines, tennis courts, video shop, and off-licence and actually go to class once in a while. Trudging past the recycling bins, the only splash of colour and verve in the compound's bleak exterior, she finds herself in a small but alarmingly dark wood, fairly reeking of moss. A well-beaten but unmarked trail leads to the head of some steps, and these down to a sunken way, damp and misty even in the heat of summer. Past an old wellhead, lichen-covered and ruinous, the

This gate, from Seaton House, is now incorporated in the university's Catholic chaplaincy.

way slopes gently downward, and in minutes she has descended 100 vertical feet or more to the immense table-like flatness of Seaton Park. Though not actually below sea level, the park's pronounced bowl will sometimes fill up with cloud, and frost over when other parts of the burgh refrain.

As likely as not, there will be no other human being within 200 yards, but the lawns and geometric flowerbeds, exploding with Technicolor blooms, look as if they were weeded moments before and trimmed by a presidential hairstylist, even now about to jump out from behind a bush to demand an outrageous but well-deserved sum. 'Who is this for?' the student asks herself. 'Can this be for me?'

At this point, the twin octagonal spires of St Machar's Cathedral become visible, more mid-twentieth-century science fiction than late medieval, topping what appears to be a sheer cliff on the park's southern edge. But the garden and its paths allow for no alternative interpretations: that is where you are going. The last few yards of the re-ascent are murderously steep, and at the top the cathedral is seen in full, surrounded by graves. Stone urns draped in stone shrouds stab the sky.

For a street obviously so old, the Chanonry is almost absurdly long, straight, and wide. Chanonry Lodge's garden wall is long and thick to match, with a forbidding ridge of sharp slates at approximately neck height (illustrated, p.158). Though bulging and meandering with age, the wall would be a militarily significant obstacle even now. Interrupted only by the impossibly small prettiness of Mitchell

Hospital, the street's giant private houses would not look out of place in federal-period New England – except for the fact that they are constructed of solid rock. There are almost never any cars here.

Across St Machar Drive – a street busy only by lost-city standards – one finds the part of the Old Town believed, albeit wrongly, to be wholly owned by King's College. This is the High Street seen from the north, with its flaring former marketplace, once again marked by the cross and terminating at the front door of the Town House, long used as the basis of the logo of the Scottish Georgian Society. It was built at a time when the government insisted on calling Scotland 'North Britain', and demanded that unionist imagery – such as 'roses and thistles growing on one stalk', and the running white horse of Hanover – be used on nearly everything. Thus it is all the more surprising to see, prominently displayed on the eastern exterior wall, a large carving of the tressure flory counter-flory and lion rampant of the old kings of Scots (illustrated, p.159). Jacobite sentiments are still encountered here, in and out of the classroom, but republican and unionist ones are equally strong; thankfully, arguments about politics remain rare. As it has been for 500 years, the people of Old Aberdeen know how to agree to disagree.

The environment has become a kind of meta-issue, filling and replacing conventional politics almost at the speed of thought; a Fair Trade campus and city are among the results. At the Fair Trade café held weekly in the university chaplaincy, one encounters students of many nations. Throughout the college, one is struck both by this internationalism and by its patchiness: Luxemburgers, Germans and Finns are

encountered all the time, Australians almost never. In many classrooms, a bare plurality of students will be Scots, a bare majority British. Irish students are disproportionately drawn to Aberdeen for reasons they seldom express. One also finds scores of Americans, not on a year-abroad scheme, but enrolled for their whole four-year degree. The great Scottish diaspora of the eighteenth and nineteenth centuries has something, but not everything, to do with this. By and large, everyone is calm, friendly and polite. Litter and vandalism are virtually unknown, such is the obvious sense that the Old Town is *for us*.

The first thing about today's student population which would have astonished Hector Boece is how many of them there are – about 14,000, over 300 times the original intake. The second would be the dawning realisation that half of them are female.

If we continue this little thought-experiment and imagine Boece in conversation with some students of today, his biggest surprise of all would be an intellectual one. In the world as it was at the close of the fifteenth century, learning was very unified. True, a mediciner had a different body of professional knowledge from a theologian, but there was still an enormous amount of common ground between one learned individual and another, whatever his particular avocation. This is no longer the case. Above all, the proliferation of the sciences would astonish a

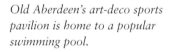

Old Aberdeen's art-deco sports pavilion is home to a popular swimming pool.

Renaissance man in one way and the invention of the social sciences and business studies would astonish him in another.

Universities have always tended to be spearheads of social change, and Aberdeen as it is today is a massively different institution from the foundations of the fifteenth century. Yet graduating students still sing the great thirteenth-century anthem of their kind, with all the Middle Ages' acute sense of the intensity of present joy in a fleeting and transitory world:

> *Gaudeamus igitur*
> *Juvenes dum sumus*
> *Post jucundum juventutem*
> *Post molestam senectutem*
> *Nos habebit humus.*

> *Let us rejoice, then,*
> *While we are young*
> *After joyful youth,*
> *After anxious old age,*
> *The grave will have us.*

Hardly any of them know what it means, but it is as joyful a noise as it ever was, and of course, as true. The graduating ceremony, in which gowned students self-consciously stumble onto the stage of Marischal College to be ritually capped by a presiding dignitary, has clear connections with medieval ceremonies of fealty. Such moments can be cherished for creating a rare sense of continuity and connectedness with a grand tradition, the more so because they are rare.

Further Reading

The charters of the burgh, extracts from the council register down to 1625, selections from the letters, guildry and treasurer's accounts, Hector Boece's account of the bishops of Aberdeen, the Bishops' Register, some of the university records, and James Gordon's *Description of Both Towns of Aberdeen* have all been published by the Spalding Club. Documentation of more purely university interest, such as the roll of alumni, has been published by the University of Aberdeen, and many minor points of interest are covered by the *Aberdeen University Review*. The Friends of St Machar's Cathedral also issue a series of occasional papers which offer a wealth of knowledge on the history of the cathedral. The suggestions below are for readers who would like to know more, but who do not want material in original languages intended for specialists.

Anderson, P.J., ed., *Studies in the History and Development of the University of Aberdeen* (Aberdeen: Aberdeen University Press, 1906)

Anderson, R.D., *The Student Community at Aberdeen, 1860–1939* (Aberdeen: Aberdeen University Press, 1988)

Brogden, W.A., *Aberdeen: An Illustrated Architectural Guide* (Edinburgh: Scottish Academic Press, 1986)

Carter, J. and McLaren, C.A., *Crown and Gown, 1495–1995* (Aberdeen: Aberdeen University Press, 1994)

Carter, J. and Pittock, J., ed., *Aberdeen and the Enlightenment* (Aberdeen: Aberdeen University Press, 1987)

Dennison, E.P., Ditchburn, D. and Lynch, M., *Aberdeen before 1800: A New History* (East Linton: Tuckwell Press, 2002)

Geddes, J., ed., *King's College Chapel, Aberdeen, 1500–2000* (Leeds: Northern Universities Press, 2000)

Harper, M., *Emigration from North-East Scotland*, 2 vols (Aberdeen: Aberdeen University Press, 1988)

Macfarlane, L., *King's College, Old Aberdeen, a Guide and History* (Aberdeen, Aberdeen University Press, 1982)

Macfarlane, L., *William Elphinstone and the Kingdom of Scotland* (Aberdeen: Aberdeen University Press, 1995)

McLaren, C.A., *Aberdeen Students, 1600–1860* (Aberdeen: University of Aberdeen, 2005)

Morgan, D., *The Villages of Aberdeen: The Spital* (Aberdeen: Denburn Books, 1996)

Morgan, D., *The Villages of Aberdeen: The Spital Lands from Sunnyside to Pittodrie* (Aberdeen: Denburn Books, 1997)

Morgan, D., *The Villages of Aberdeen: Old Aberdeen* (Aberdeen: Denburn Books, 2000)

Orem, W.T., *Description of the Chanonry, Cathedral and King's College of Old Aberdeen, 1724–25* (London: J. Nichols, 1782, and other editions)

Smith, J.S., ed., *New Light on Medieval Aberdeen* (Aberdeen, Aberdeen University Press, 1985)

Smith, J.S., ed., *Old Aberdeen: Bishops, Burghers and Buildings* (Aberdeen: Aberdeen University Press, 1991)

Stones, J.A., ed., *A Tale of Two Burghs: the Archaeology of Old and New Aberdeen* (Aberdeen: Art Gallery and Museum, 1987)

Todd, S., *The Cathedral Church of St Machar, Old Aberdeen* (Derby: Pilgrim Press, 1988)

Trail, K.E., *The Story of Old Aberdeen* (Aberdeen: D. Wyllie & Son, 1929)

Trail, K.E., *Reminiscences of Old Aberdeen* (Aberdeen: D. Wyllie & Son, 1932)

Acknowledgements

The authors and editors of *The Lost City: Old Aberdeen* are grateful for the generous support of Petro-Canada, which was instrumental in bringing this project to fruition.

We would also like to thank Chris Banks, Anna Brown, Jennifer Carter, James Claffey OP, Kirstie Ellington, Chris Gane, Jane Geddes, Kieran German, Martyn Gorman, Stan Jack, Lori Manders and her staff, Ralph O'Connor, Bruce Purdon, Alison Saunders, Sarah Singleton, Atholl Wing, The Friends of Aberdeen University Library, Aberdeen University Museums Service, Photographic Services, Historic Collections, and Special Libraries and Archives, the Aberdeen University Alumnus Association, and all of the people and businesses of Old Aberdeen for helping to make this book possible.

The Photographs

All colour photographs in this book are by and copyright David Langan, except as follows.

The photograph on page vi is by Robert Watson.

The photographs on pages 1 (bottom), 3, 5, 7, 9, 11 (right), 17 (right), 22 (top row), 25, 49, 53, 56, 66, 75, 79, 80, 87 (right), 115, 122, 123, 124 (top right), 137, 149, 153, 155, 156, 157, 159, 160 are by Marie Shaw.

The images on pages 12, 28, 29, 32, 34, 35, 47, 48, 76, 77, 78, 81, 82 (left), 83, 86, 87 (left), 88, 89, 92, 93, 94, 96, 98, 102, 105, 106, 107, 108, 109, 110, 112, 114, 116, 119, 120, 121, 129, 130, 131, 133, 134, 141, and 146 were furnished from the collections of the University of Aberdeen.

The photographs on pages 26, 85 and 152 are by Eric Ellington.

Those on pages 64 and 82 (right) are reproduced by permission of the Trustees of the National Library of Scotland.

Those on pages 138 and 139 are by Eleanor Hayes.

The final image, page 163, is by Chris Banks.